VISIONS IN THE STONE

Visions
in the
Stone

Journey to the
Source of Hidden Knowledge

E. J. GOLD

GATEWAYS/IDHHB PUBLISHERS

Frontispiece photo by Philip Stark, NYC
In this photo, Mr. Gold is wearing blue chalcedony
Sumerian beads dating from the 3rd millenium B.C.

The illustrations opposite the title pages of chapters two through
thirteen of this book are 19th Century depictions of Arab life.

Copyright ©1989 by E.J. Gold
All Rights Reserved. Printed in the U.S.A.
First Printing.

Published by:
GATEWAYS / IDHHB, INC.
PO Box 370, Nevada City, CA 95959, (916) 477-1116

Some of the material in this book first appeared as a privately published edition, *Volume IV* of the *Secret Talks with G.* series, ©1980.

Library of Congress Cataloging-in-Publication Data
Gold, E.J.
    Visions in the stone : journey to the source of hidden knowledge / E.J. Gold.
        p. cm.
    Includes index.
    ISBN 0-89556-082-8- -ISBN 0-89556-057-7 (pbk.) : $14.50
    1. Psychometry (Occultism) 2. Iraq—Antiquities. 3. Iraq—Description and travel. 4. Gold, E.J.—Journeys—Iraq.
I. Title.
BF1286.G66 1989
133.8—dc20   89-1440
                                                      CIP

To
Henry Anavian
with gratitude.

TABLE OF CONTENTS

PREFACE

This challenging book calls into question apparently mundane and obvious basic assumptions we have about life and reality. If we are not ready to revise our most cherished beliefs we will find it devastatingly difficult to embark on this wonderful archaeological travelogue which culminates in some of the most fascinatingly esoteric material ever revealed.

Like anyone else in his position, Gold has faced hundreds and thousands of times the perennial question, "What is the source of your knowledge?" But when he said that his knowledge could be traced back to the Babylonians, little did I suspect precisely how he had obtained it when I asked him that question six years ago on a New York street during a break at a shamanic workshop.

In this follow-up to *The Human Biological Machine as a Transformational Apparatus* and *Life in the Labyrinth* where he lays his ground work, Gold boldly and candidly describes some of the techniques which enabled him to unlock secrets transmitted from highly evolved shamen of the Sumerian-Babylonian lineage.

The methods he describes and invites us to try involve psychometry, the innate psionic ability to see, hear and feel scenes from the ancient past by extracting visions from ancient artifacts. Although this is unusual it is actually not that surprising. For example, a number of archaeologists have turned to a very esoteric branch of psychics in order to locate buried artifacts at archaeological digs around Flagstaff, Arizona, and many other indigenous sites in North America. So this is only one step further than what is being explored by respected scientists in related fields. Actually the use of psychometry is less shocking than the statement that ancient shamen *intentionally* encoded data in artifacts. This is where he really goes out on a limb.

To understand or even be willing to accept that psychometry can be a valid method for obtaining knowledge, one has to grasp that the macro-dimensional nature of reality is literal. This opens up unexpected avenues which the author has thoroughly explored. He goes far beyond the stultified and monodimensional vision offered to us today by the dominant materialistic world-view.

Visions in the Stone is not limited to the world of immediate appearances but shows how borders between lower and higher dimensions can be bridged. The bridge begins at the lower end of the spectrum with "reading artifacts" all the way to the other end with direct intercession of "higher entities" in macro-dimensional spheres.

According to Gold, "spiritual contamination" by exposure to reading artifacts was invented by individuals organized in schools possessing higher—

now esoteric—knowledge. There is however a Catch-22. In order to unlock artifacts left by schools one needs to know something about invocation. But objective invocation is something that one learns only in a school. This means that these secrets can only be discovered by someone who is already in possession of great knowledge. For those who don't have the knowledge and understanding, and who work through crude trial and error methods, such as modern astrology and mediumship, it is pure gibberish, and the secret keeps itself.

Not only did such things occur in the past; they are occuring today. School artifacts are being produced and seeded into the world at large by contemporary schools which encrypt in them certain data and transform them into emitting artifacts. Most people are sensitive to these recordings but very few have any idea of what they are responding to.

This implies that spiritual initiation and transformation do not solely originate in the individual but begin with gentle influences which coax us toward the path over a long period of time. A certain amount of randomness is at play in determining who receives these radiations. But accidental exposure to influences from higher sources can only give us a taste for something we will have to work for to achieve on our own.

Having personally worked with antiquities and visited countless museums around the world I came to thrive on the unusual psychic experiences I began to expect when visiting museums with ancient artifacts—particularly of the Sumerian culture. I knew without a shred of doubt that the artifacts were altering and expanding my consciousness, and I became very addicted to this. The idiosyncratic organic responses to these subtle radiations range from queasiness, dizziness, vertigo, irritability, agitation, nausea, uneasiness, to a feeling of elation, excitement or bliss, as Joseph Campbell uses the word. Readers will perhaps recall strange sensations associated with museum visits and visits to ancient sites....

Once one is attuned to these emanations, they can be so powerful that it becomes difficult to endure them for a long period of time. Eventually I found myself less and less able to visit museums replete with reading artifacts for any great length of time. I would soon feel utterly exhausted much as one can imagine a medium being exhausted after a seance. Of course I didn't have the operant mechanism figured out, but I knew that the artifacts were acting on me and that certain cultures had more impact than others, Western Asiatic displays being especially powerful.

As an experiment I recently mentioned the idea of emitting artifacts to a person who would be considered enlightened by late-twentieth-century standards, and was met with an expression of shock, horror and indignation. In all fairness I must admit that if I did not myself have first-hand experience of such things I would probably also find it hard to believe that in this day and age such things as esoteric information recorded in artifacts are possible. But exposure to a great number of strange phenomena related to these artifacts has taught me differently.

The discoveries related in this book cannot be made in the state of walking sleep, nor can they be made through any ordinary means, no matter how exalted. These discoveries can only be the result of correctly directed and precisely guided spiritual transformation and the exercise of higher centers which are unlocked through prolonged work on self.

The esoteric secrets that have been forgotten for hundreds of years would never have resurfaced if not for E.J. Gold's uncanny expertise as a labyrinthine voyager and his ability to interact with macrodimensional worlds interpenetrating the human realm. It took a rare combination of scientist, adventurer, and shaman to uncover what has eluded humanity since the Dark Ages.

Gold has accomplished what most individuals only dream of and, moreover, he shows *how he did it.* He demonstrates that in the long run, we become whatever it is that we strive for through our own efforts... beneficial influences gently guiding us along but never replacing personal effort, persistance, cunning, and individual suffering.

The very fact that this book has been written offers hope that we can free ourselves from the stupidity, arrogance, blindness, vanity, corruption, fear, selfishness, and all the other deadly enemies that feed on us and eat away at our only chance at real life.

This book is deadly serious in spite of all the disguises and amusing detours intended to playfully distract us from the clarity and directness of its message and fortify our attention and intention. This is not a fanciful allegory, or the strange product of an overly active imagination. It is just about as straightforward as any competent introduction to shamanism can be. Of course the author is probably betting that very few of us will actually try what he is proposing, so why not say it clearly, and he's probably right....

However, for the few who, amidst the growing sense of doom in this late twentieth century, are tired of ordinary life, who want to change and who are willing to really work at it, spiritual transformation is not some abstract dream. It has more reality than our sleepfilled lives. It is so tangible that one can almost measure how it changes one's relationship to the very stuff of which the universe is made. The knowledge that, once awakened and transformed into an active electrical field without impinging anomalies, we will be guided by higher knowledge and able to blend and work within other greater electrical fields, serves as a beacon until a world with receded limits unfolds itself to us, the real world which is veiled today by sleep.

But as Gold points out this can only happen through self-initiation. In the end we are on our own and it is strictly by our own efforts that we will arrive at anything. We must find the inner strength and necessity which will give us the momentum to persist on our path.

Linda Corriveau,
Editor and Museologist

INTRODUCTION

by Robert Anton Wilson

*Once in Afghanistan, our expedition lost the cork-screw
and we had to survive for over two weeks on nothing
but food and water.*

—Claude William Dunkenfield[1]

Let there be no mistake about it: the book you
hold in your hands is as dangerous as a letter-bomb.
It might blow your head off.

Perhaps I can explain that warning with a
parable. As all students of Irish literature know, the
late Sir Myles na gCopaleen[2] (1869-1968) became
enamored, in his old age, of the verse of Dylan
Thomas. In 1966, despite his four score and 18 years
and an advanced case of paresis, Sir Myles departed
on a hazardous[3] journey across the Irish Sea, from
Dun Laoghaire to Hollyhead, to explore the dark,

eldritch hills of Wales and find the fabulous church mentioned in Thomas' famous *Ballad of the Long-Legged Bait*—the cathedral with the "talkative seven tombs" through which an anchor had dived to reveal an underground "metropolis of fishes" where the Fisherman stood at the door of his home "with his long-legged heart in his hand."

Sincere, dedicated, intrepid, Sir Myles wandered endlessly, from Llareggub[4] to Swansea, from Llakcuf to Taliesen, but never did he find sight, evidence or even rumor of such a surreal citadel. Eventually, exhausted and embittered, the old man returned to Ireland, where he wrote his last anguished book, **a chara, no caith tabac**[5], a bitter diatribe against Dylan Thomas in particular and the race of versifiers and rhymesters in general, a breed he described as "liars, loons, pansies, ding-alings, wallbangers and drunks at best, and charlatans in their secret hearts." It has been granted by even the hostile von Hanfkopf[6] that no more damaging criticism of the mythopoetic mind has been written since the early days of Logical Positivism.

Dejected and despairing, Sir Myles might have died a bitter old man. But one night in 1968, during a particularly horrendous Irish thunder storm, all the lights in his castle went out, and Sir Myles went down to the basement alone—his butler was drunk, and the caretaker had become a hopeless Ketamine freak—in an attempt to reset the fuse box. Wandering in the subterranean depths, with only a flickering candle to guide him, Sir Myles began to hear *slurping* footsteps and strange *teratological* grunts and gargles in the surrounding dark. He sensed the presence of something beyond the ken of normal human experience: something unspeakable and unthinkable. He felt a sudden clammy breath on the back of his neck and turned, very slowly, peering into the thick, unpulsating darkness.

And then he saw It—

But Finn O'Brien, in his great biography of Sir Myles, tells that story much better than I could.[7]

Who has ears, let them hear.

II

We're all in this alone.

—Lily Tomlin

Let us, as the Chinese say, draw our chairs closer to the fire and examine what we think we are talking about.

All epics take the form of a Quest. Usually, the hero undergoes an Underground Journey, or a visit to the Realm of Thud where he is afflicted by buzzing and whistling Things from the Pink Dimension, or is somehow violently wrenched from tribal "consensus reality." Parcifal had Chapel Perilous. Christ, Osiris, Tim Finnegan and Sherlock Holmes died and rose again. Dante spent a lot of time wandering through the corridors of Hell before he caught his first glimpse of Paradise. Odysseus had his own trip to Hades. Jack Nicholson had to go back to Chinatown again even though he foresaw that "You never know what's going on down there." Luke Skywalker had to go into that Dark Platonic Cave and see his own kinship with Darth Vader, etc.[8]

Since the Dawn of Humanity, this archetypal Quest has been the subject of myth, legend, poetry, novels and **Elephant Doody Comix.** As a traditional American spiritual tells us,

Jesus walked this lonesome valley
He had to walk there all alone
Nobody else could do it for him
He had to go there all alone

The possible rewards of the Quest outweigh the certain dangers and discomforts: but these blessings come at unexpected times, in unimaginable ways. As even the skeptical Marx noted, "If you say the Magic Word, the duck will come down and give you $100."

Descending into the abyss of lost history and the deeper chasm of the collective unconscious, E.J. Gold here takes us on a Quest much like the adventures of Parcifal or Sir Myles' search for the Mystic Cathedral which he only found, like the bluebird of happiness, in his own backyard—or, at least, in his basement. Along the way he teaches us how to read "the signature of all things" that Stephen Dedalus sought on the beach of Sandymount in Joyce's **Ulysses.**[9]

Who has eyes, let them see.

III

*That is not dead which can eternal lie
And with strange Aeons ever death may die.*

—**Abdul Alhazred**[10]

Lately I dream a lot about the late, great science-fiction writer, Philip K. Dick. Phil had a vision, toward the end of his life, in which he realized that all humanity is held captive in a Black Iron Prison. (Comparisons with Plato's Cave are egregious and odious.) The Prison, he discovered, was part of the Roman Empire, which had never ended: 2000 years of False History had been inserted into our brains, to keep us from remembering that we are living in the Time of the Messiah.

In horrible detail, Dick realized that Nero and Caligula and their kin still govern us, wearing false masks and pretending to be named Nixon or Reagan.[11] The Christians are being thrown to the lions every day, but we retain only distorted images of what is happening—the "mysterious" deaths of John and Bobby and Martin, etc. To destroy the Gnosis, the Empire has not only erased real memories, inserted false memories and built the Black Iron Prison, but has also hidden from us the knowledge that "the Buddha is in the park." If we can only remember that phrase every day, and meditate on it until we understand it, we can all escape from the Black Iron Prison.

"The Buddha is in the park." What the deuce does that mean?

Sixty years earlier an analogous vision was granted to Aleister Crowley. Uncle Al (as we call him, down at Illuminati headquarters) saw that the world is governed by the Lord of the Abyss of Hallucinations, who continually shouts, "Truth! Truth! Truth!" This Abyss, Crowley was given to know, is also called, among humans, "Hell" or "the Universe"[12] or "Consciousness."

Even earlier, William Blake perceived in Deep Vision that Dark Satanic Mills had been constructed to hide the places where "the Holy Lamb of God" had walked. Specifically calling for "arrows of desire" and "chariots of fire," he vowed to rebuild Jerusalem in England's grim unpleasant land.

Maybe he was another nut case?

Down there in the basement that dark night in 1968—it was March 17, actually: St. Patrick's Day[13]— Sir Myles found himself confronting a chimpanzee. Lithe, sinewy, dynamic, the little fellow was dressed in a green tuxedo and wearing a green silk hat. (I have decided that maybe I can tell this story almost as well as O'Brien did.)

"O Seeker of the Truth," the chimpanzee said, "leave sinful Dublin. Go to Chicago, to the address I will give you on Lake Shore Drive, and there you will find the goal of your Quest. Just knock on the door and ask for Lucy Smythe Danforth." And he handed Sir Myles a card with the address 2323 Lake Shore Drive and the scribbled words, "Land safely, darling."

From that day forward, Sir Myles was transformed. He rented his castle to some rich Americans (Larry and Susie Davis) and made out his final will (with the solicitors Locke, Standish, Downey on Lower Skerries Drive). He packed a small bag and departed at once on Aer Lingus (nonstop flight Dublin to New York, first class).

In Manhattan, Sir Myles visited briefly with an old friend, Liam S. Dooley, and then boarded Amtrak for Chicago. Lustfully, suspensefully, desperately he counted the hours as the train huffed and puffed across New Jersey and even more dreary parts of the American LandScaped Dream. That night in the diner he could eat no more than lamb stew and dumplings, with a snort of Larson's Scotch and Drambuie.

Finally, the train arrived in Chicago and Sir Myles looked about him at the city's sinister lights and sights and delights. "Like Satan's Domain," he thought apprehensively. Then he hopped a cab and sped like a flaming arrow to his destination on Lake Shore Drive.

He knocked on the door, and it was opened by an obviously wealthy middle-aged woman—her butler was drunk, too, and her caretaker was strung out on speed.

"Lucy Smythe Danforth?" Sir Myles asked eagerly.

"Yes? But have I had the privilege...?"

"The chimpanzee sent me!" Sir Myles cried.

"Chimpanzee?" the woman exclaimed. "I don't know any fucking chimpanzees, mister. It's bad enough we got Nigrahs living next door!" And she slammed the door, and Sir Myles was Enlightened.

He stood there for 23 long minutes—laughing, sobbing, devastated.

He turned and could suddenly read the signature of all things.

Like Stephen Dedalus.

Let us summarize:

Seekers find only what they are ready to find.

Dust-motes contain galaxies to the awakened vision.

But I have been on long enough. The next act is better. Be prepared for a weird journey and a Zen hotfoot at the end. The clues that are most obvious are the misdirections. The truth is right out in the open, where nobody wants to see it.

NOTES

1. This great American philosopher and sociologist was posthumously canonized by the First Church of Satan in San Francisco, but he was dead at the time and couldn't make his objections known.

2. Although well-known to all students of Literature, Science and Demonology in Ireland, Sir Myles has not received due appreciation in America. The standard biography is Finn O'Brien's **Myles**

Away From the English (Poolbeg Press, Dublin, 1973). The serious student will also wish to consult LaFournier's **na gCopaleen: Homme ou Dieu?** (University of Paris, 1975), LaTournier's **na g-Copalien: l'Enigme de l'Occident** (Editions J'ai Lu, Paris, 1976) and Vinkinoog's **De Onbekende Filosoof** (De Kosmos, Amsterdam, 1978). The venomous and unfounded diatribes of von Hanfkopf **(na gCopeleen macht eine grosse Dummheit,** University of Heidelberg, 1981) can well be ignored. Sir Myles was an initiate of the Hermetic Order of the Golden Dawn, translated the Finn Mac-Cumhal epic into Homeric Greek ("to make it even more incomprehensible to the English") and founded the Royal Sir Myles na gCopaleen Paleo-Anthropological Institute, the Royal Sir Myles na gCopaleen Psycho-Pharmacological Institute and the Royal Sir Myles na gCopaleen Institute of Chronotopological Studies. (Chronotopology is the study of cultural temporal relativity, inspired by Einstein and anthropology. Sir Myles's main contribution to this field was his demonstration that while Irish Gaelic contains 23 synonyms for *mañana*, none of them express that precise degree of urgency.)

3. Because the employees of Sealink were on strike that month and the company had hired as strikebreakers a group of Rastafarians hurriedly rounded up in the pubs of Liverpool. These enthusiastic but inexperienced sailors alarmed the Irish passengers by their sinister "dreadlocks," the thick fogs of cannabis vapor exhaled from their pipes and their habit of haranguing everybody about Jesus being Black and the Pope being "Imperial Wizard of

the Ku Klux Klan, Godfather of the Mafia and General All-Around Anti-Christ."

4. The town that was the setting for Dylan Thomas's verse-play, **Under Milk Wood**, a title which for sheer Celtic obscurity rivals **At Swim-Two-Birds**, the celebrated magical allegory written by Sir Myles under the pen-name "Flann O'Brien." (The fact that Sir Myles used the pen-name Flann O'Brien and that his first biographer was Finn O'-Brien does not demonstrate von Hanfkopf's absurd thesis that Sir Myles wrote his own biography under a pen-name, just to glorify himself. If Sir Myles created O'Brien, how could O'Brien have created Sir Myles?)

5. Sir Myles explained to cronies at the Starry Plough pub in Dublin that he wrote this work in Gaelic, "a language nobody reads," because he had a thesis "nobody will want to hear."

6. The hermetic La Puta claims (**La Estupidad de von Hanfkopf**, University of Madrid, 1987) that von Hanfkopf, who claimed O'Brien was a pen-name for Sir Myles, was himself a Masque, another pen-name for Sir Myles, who thus allegedly wrote both a glorification of himself and a denunciation of himself after faking his death in the eldritch "Kerry *pookah*" incident. This thesis is ill-documented and Byzantine.

7. O'Brien, *op. cit.* p. 666.

8. Contrary to popular belief, the so-called "water rat" is not a rat, at all; it is a vole. (I just put this in for those who are actually reading the footnotes.)

9. As Sir Myles wrote in his early and little-known **Listen, Stephen Dedalus: Leopold Sum-**

mons Divinity (Dalkey Archives, Dublin, 1933), the first sentence of **Ulysses** has 22 words, each of which corresponds to a letter of the Hebrew alphabet, a Trump of the Tarot, a chapter in the Book of Revelations and a path on the Cabalistic Tree of Life. E.g. the first word of the sentence is "Stately," because the first Hebrew letter, *aleph,* means ox and Joyce regarded Statesmen as cattle, the corresponding Tarot card is the Fool because only Fools put their faith in the rulers of this world, etc. The last word of the sentence is "crossed" because the last Hebrew letter, *Tau,* means cross, the corresponding Tarot card is The World (where we are all crucified), etc. But the progression from "Stately" to "crossed" intimates the "two Masters" Stephen Dedalus later says he serves, the State and the Church, which are then parodied in Buck Mulligan's ribald songs *Coronation Day* and *The Ballad of Joking Jesus.* Sir Myles neglected to note that Stephen Dedalus is 22 years old in the novel, and the other hero, Leopold Bloom, is identified with Shakespeare; Shakespeare's son died at 11 years and Bloom's son at 11 days ($2 \times 11 = 22$). Blake asserted he saw "infinity in a grain of sand," but works like **Ulysses** and the present tome attempt to make us see it, too.

    10. Sir Myles was of the school of Islamic studies which holds that "the mad poet Abdul Alhazred" was not really mad at all. Indeed, as Price has written (**A Critical Commentary on the Necronomicon**, Cryptic Publications, 1988), the Arabian word, *quok'ou,* often applied to Alhazred only loosely means "mad" and also has such connotations as "intoxicated," "enchanted" "gifted with poetic vision" or "stoned out of one's gourd" (among other things).

Etymologically, the term originally signifies one who hears the Djinns singing and carousing all night in the desert. Sir Myles believed Alhazred "had a heavy hasheesh habit" but "was as sane as most people in that part of the world."

11. RONALD WILSON REAGAN has 6 letters in his first name, 6 in his middle name, and 6 in his last name. 666. See?

12. Bishop George Berkeley (1685-1753) proved that the universe doesn't exist but God thinks that it does. Like Sir Myles, he was an Irishman.

13. That was the day the Irish Republican Army blew up the statue of Lord Nelson on O'Connell Street. Although nobody was killed in the incident, Dubliners still consider it another I.R.A. atrocity because it ruined a favorite Dublin joke—the observation that the biggest street in the most Catholic country in the world had a statue of an adulterer at its head (O'Connell), another adulterer in the middle (Nelson) and a third adulterer at the foot (Parnell).

VISIONS IN THE STONE

E.J. Gold, *Moonstruck,* Monoprint,
11" x 15", Rives BFK, 1987.

Chapter One

THE MEETING

Finding a labyrinth guide in the hustle and bustle of contemporary cities can happen in the most innocuous places...such as the next table over, at Alex's Borscht Bowl.

A cold day in January. New York City, 1959. Uptown on the west side of Broadway, between Seventy-fourth and Seventy-fifth street, stands a turn-of-the-century brownstone building; the Ansonia Hotel.

Rent by the month or lease by the year, the hotel overflows with White Russian immigrants, mostly opera and ballet performers. Wading through vocalizations, piano arpeggios and echoing arias, down the elevator and past the challenging bulk of the doormen, I step through the brass trimmed doors and turn right.

A momentary stop at the Tip-Toe-Inn bakery and delicatessen. Take a number, then find a line and stand in it. Five lines across, twenty people deep. Unknowingly, this unassuming bakery is the pilot project, the prototype, for all the more interesting rides yet to be installed at Disneyland...just another new amusement park in California.

A grim, intimidating, robotically rapid stride past dead and angry faces, toward the subway on seventy-second street; descend the dripping wet stone steps, drop a dime, ram myself through the turnstile and wait.

Cold, wet clammy wind in my face. A deep rumbling sound announces the arrival of another rattling iron train which swallows me with its hungry and impatient doors, hurtles me downtown, and spits me out in a boiling crowd of ant-like, busy androids.

Cutting through the crowd, pushing past the revolving bars, past somber despairing zombies, climbing upward on old, worn granite stairs I emerge from the tomblike tunnel; propelled slightly by the gentle pressure of underground air, I thread my way through narrow winding West Village streets to a small basement restaurant; Alex's Borscht Bowl.

The subdued muttering of pre-revolutionary chess masters bemoaning the fate of the Romanoffs. A strange esoteric brotherhood of unknowable, inscrutable Russians. How could these pathetic creatures be the immortal Hidden Guides for whom I had searched for so long? Endless chess games, continual hypnagogic prattle, recounting and reliving and regretting and restructuring the past, all belie this deduction.

A penned note scrawled in faded brown ink on the flyleaf of a Louis Elziveer text, The History of Rome, in an eighteenth century hand supplies me with the clue I need.

The Hidden Guides, gatekeepers and keepers of the keys to...to what? Something called the Labyrinth, about which I know nothing, remember nothing. Then why this gnawing hunger?

Crackling warmth of the stone-captured fire, shadows dancing on the far wall as they sit absorbed in their eternal games, ignoring, rejecting any overture, leaving no opening, no options. Yet here they are before me. How to break that cold, killing silence, that impenetrable wall of deadly indifference?

Many weeks of patient searching, and now this. But that makes perfect sense. After all, if they were all that easy to find, why would they be called "hidden"?

Sitting in silence, huddled alone at a corner table, waiting for the entrance of some Hidden Guides, who, according to my calculations, ought to be wearing brown monks' robes so they can be easily distinguished from ordinary mortals.

I knew that these people sitting here could not possibly be the Guides, and the reason I knew this was that if they were Guides, they'd be out working somewhere, guiding someone, or something.

Who ever heard of guides who don't guide? But maybe they are guides. Maybe there just isn't anyone to guide any more. Maybe no one is interested in the Labyrinth in these cynical days.

After all, our contemporary civilization has become so superior and advanced that, thanks to scientists, doctors, and educators, everyone already knows exactly what they can do and exactly what they can do with it.

As I sat here mentally picking my nose, scratching my ass, tapping one foot and wiggling the other, nodding my head and imperceptibly twiddling my spoon in my potato soup with my left hand while scrawling these notes with my right, trying my damndest to be ambidextrous as hell, I couldn't help but be dimly aware that somehow, a definite sensation of anger had been slowly welling up inside, seeping unnoticeably from my madly-racing headbrain and spilling septically into the leach-line of my heart.

I happened to know that it was my headbrain that was the root and cause of it all, because the headbrain functions by association, which is to say, one thing suggests another, and that's exactly what seemed to be happening.

But that didn't explain the anger. I needed guiding, and these guides were ignoring my needs. Yes, that must be what the anger was about. But was it really prudent of me to just waltz up to them and confront them about this? Not without knowing the precise extent of their powers, it wasn't. They might poof me right out of existence for my presumption.

Well, this must be what it's like to formulate your first Real Aim In Life, and my first Real Aim was, at the moment, to somehow become as powerful as the Hidden Guides, so I could safely accuse them of goofing off.

Chapter Two

ON THE ROAD TO POWER

Karima managed to relate to me the following information between rapid bursts of automatic weaponfire...

On the west road into Khorsabad during the holidays, an encounter with Karima, a *Ghawazi* street dancer and amateur archaeologist.

We walked side by side toward a building underneath which secret archaeological excavations were proceeding.

She understood my interest in the Hidden Guides, mentioned in a moment—actually several hours—of indiscretion.

Entering the building, we shuffled in darkness past rough plaster walls. In the dim light, I could just barely see, but it was obvious that the excavation had penetrated quite deeply beneath the floor of the little chamber.

Underneath the floor, a tunnel of dressed stone exposed by the diggings. In a niche cut by the original builders stood a finely carved alabaster jar in the late Imperial Roman style, with delicately formed high curving handles, alongside which, perfectly undamaged, lay several beautifully formed glass jars, richly patinated and glistening with brilliantly iridescent purples, reds, golds, greens, yellows and blues.

As we eagerly pried away the lid, we could hear the hiss of air and see a puff of dust in the bottom.

On the outside of the jar, deeply etched into the surface, a crudely cut inscription, inscribed—if penmanship is any indication—by a dying hand.

Come to think about it, if bad penmanship is an indication of a dying hand, then three-quarters of the high school and college students—and all the doctors—in America are already dead.

The inscription read, as nearly as I could copy:

AESCULAPIO ET SANITATI
L. CLODIUS HERMIPPUS
QUI VIXIT ANNOS CXV. DIES V.
IN SARAMOUNA
PUELLARUM ANHELITU
QUOD ETIAM POST MORTEM
EJUS NON PARUM MIRANTUR PHYSICI
JAM POSTERI SIC VITAM DUCITE

Which tells us that L. Claudius Hermippus, evidently a Roman citizen living in the Saramoung District of Kurdistan, had lived for exactly one hundred and fifteen years and five days through the breath of young women, which the writer of the ancient inscription had thought ought to be worthy of the consideration of physicians and of posterity.

Now, if we take this inscription at face value, it means that a man lived to a very advanced age through some obscure use of the hot breath exhaled by young women.

It is noteworthy that the anonymous writer has specified young women, and had notably made no mention of middle-aged and older women, nor was any mention made of exactly how this hot breath was to be extracted, and nothing comes immediately to mind.

Now, what contribution, I wondered, could the breath of young women make toward extension of the human lifespan?

"It says nothing about how a woman is to survive," Karima said drily. "Do you suppose the breath of young men is of any use in the same way for women?"

We excitedly debated whether this artifact indicated the possible existence of local accessible entrances to the Higher Dimensions and non-human sectors of the Great Labyrinth.

We spent the next several hours speculating about the possible whereabouts of the Hidden Guides, inhabitants of the Higher Dimensions who evidently wander periodically into the human sector for one obscure reason or another, nobody knows exactly what.

"Perhaps," I speculated, "they act as an assisting factor for the arising of conscious life and to prepare certain members of the human community as 'Candidates For Another Life', and also, if they show any evidence of superior intelligence, do the week's grocery shopping as long as they're in the neighborhood."

Karima mentioned in passing that most of the hidden entrances to the Labyrinth had long ago been closed due to the overenthusiasm of several million participants in countless recent martial conflicts including the Great War, the Hitler War, the Crimean War, and the Moldavian Conflict.

"But they might perhaps be opened by someone with exact knowledge," she postulated.

In the evening, during several serious scientific experiments related to the question of the use of hot breath toward longevity and immortality, Karima and I happened to stumble upon several sure-fire methods for the non-squeamish, which definitely provide both hot breath and access to the Higher Dimensions. We decide to call them *gateways*.

Somehow I managed in spite of the lack of tape recorder or notebook, to retain almost verbatim all the data I obtained from Karima on the subject.

I don't know why I remember this particular conversation more than another...perhaps as a result of the ingestion of copious amounts of *mastique* and *pita,* a pocket bread—sort of a Turkish taco—which may have accidentally-automatically associated themselves with these ideas, rooting this data in that part of my deepest consciousness ordinarily reserved exclusively for the collected erotic memories associated with the ingestion of extravagant foods.

Months earlier, she had been presented with a souvenir bullet from the Battle of Gallipoli. She was accustomed to carry this very same bullet in her left breast pocket.

Just as we left the building, sudden violence erupted between Nestorian Christians and Shiite Moslems. In this respect, it was a completely ordinary day in the Middle East.

But before we could take refuge from the battle, she was struck in the chest by a nine-pound hardbound, metal-trimmed Old Heidelberg edition of the Standard Unexpurgated Family Bible With Apocrypha, burdened with the additional weight of one-hundred and seventeen pages of family photographs and a complete genealogical chart going all the way back to the Middle Ages.

Ironically, had she not carried that bullet in the usual place, that infernal Bible would surely have penetrated the rib cage, killing her instantly.

She managed somehow to relate to me the following information between rapid bursts of automatic weaponfire:

"All surviving entrances to the Higher Dimensions are piled with heaps of rubbish.

"Only very disturbed persons such as ourselves would seriously consider performing the necessary ablutions to clear away the garbage from these entrances to the Higher Dimensions.

"It is the custom of human beings in the mainstream of life to block up these entrances if found, and to destroy anyone who might be likely to indicate their whereabouts to others.

"They fear the Higher Dimensions and have for centuries characterized the inhabitants of Higher Dimensions as bizarre creatures who steal their children, sour their milk, and destroy crops and, in general, create various forms of petty mischief. The fact is, their mischief is far from petty.

"It is rare for people from the mainstream of human life to find a Higher Dimension entrance without help of some kind—even if this help is invisible to the ordinary eye.

"We are guided to the entrances to the Higher Dimensions by a series of seemingly accidental coincidences, evidently contrived somehow by Hidden Guides.

"It is sometimes possible that those remaining accessible gateways to the Higher Dimensions may become visible to an individual who has had his inner sight opened by some unusual circumstance...or by sex," she added, her lips pursed in a cute smirk which spelled disaster for any plans to continue our study of the excavation before morning.

"In this case, the markings which describe the path to the Higher Dimensions—ravaged though they may be by the passage of time and the destructive urges of wild animals, not the least of which is that arch-destroyer of all time, the human being—are suddenly revealed.

"However, even should we, by a series of artificially manufactured coincidences, led—hopefully unerringly—by the revealing spirit, manage to find our way into the labyrinth, the matter still remains that one must earn one's livelihood among a new, very different and unimaginably gentle people and culture.

"For this reason, before we attempt entry into the Higher Dimensions, we must be familiar with handcrafts, particularly the repair variety, without the usual corresponding feelings of loss of personal dignity so common in contemporary Western civilization.

"This is necessary because no one has special supernatural powers in the Higher Dimensions as they do in ordinary life, nor will you find among them the imaginary reincarnations of Julius Caesar, Napoleon, Nefertiti, or Cleopatra.

"Everyone is forced to earn their living in the realm of practical crafts. Paper-pushing is useless in the Higher Dimensions, and accountants do not generally do well there.

"Among the common current beliefs on the surface world about the Inner world is the widespread assumption that all Higher Dimension inhabitants just sit around staring at clouds.

"Nothing could be further from the truth. All Higher Dimension inhabitants must at all times live by their wits—tempered by their conscience—not only in the Higher Dimensions, but also when forced to wander in the lower dimensions among humans and other lower biological species.

"Living by one's wits is only attained and mastered through long apprenticeship. But to whom or what?

"Once in a while these Higher Dimension inhabitants are forced to take certain steps which become necessary due to our insistence on destroying not only ourselves—which might be a blessing in the long run—but also the planet.

"The unconscious manifestations of human primates inevitably draw off certain Higher Dimension energies which cannot be replaced.

"This occurs because of an inherent pattern of laziness, thanks to which human creatures tend to utilize sixty-cycle intermittent reversing electrical energy to power the machines which perform their labours, labours which in any case rightfully belong to the essential self.

"Humans have apparently for centuries believed that in order to preserve their emotional stability, they must allow themselves to manifest all unconscious urges freely and without restraint, regardless of the resulting destruction in the Higher Dimensions, about which they know exactly nothing and care even less.

"In the Higher Dimensions, things are different. Everyone is aware of the totality of effects in the general electrical field which permeates all worlds, and therefore all actions are taken with consideration of both their immediate and far-reaching results.

"No single human primate acting alone has sufficient force to drain the Higher Dimensions of their energy, but the combined action of all human primates is sufficient to drain away the majority of higher energies.

"As matters stand now," she said, "this valuable energy usable for the benefit of all life on the planet—and in some cases elsewhere also—is scattered out into deep space, where it is captured and eaten by certain large blue bubble-beings and their reddish consorts who exist on the outermost limits of the universe.

"The extreme cold and exposure to outer space of the surface of the earth makes it possible for this Higher Dimensional energy to be released into outer space by the process of radiation.

"In this way, the human population of earth has stripped the planet of almost all remaining energy needed for further evolution, not only of their own species, but also of all other species on earth, with the singular exception of the cockroach, which will soon be the sole survivor, just as it is on the planet *Toolkosios,* called by humans 'the planet Mars.'

"And unfortunately for the few human primates who do have a definite possibility of reaching the Higher Dimensions through one of the entrances, other surface dwellers wish to prevent this from occurring.

"Not only do some perverted human primates restrict themselves from knowledge and penetration of the Inner World, but they actively make it their business to prevent others from gaining access to the Higher Dimensions.

"It is only with conscious help from an experienced guide that those who have become caught up in the inexorable machinery of organic life have any hope of escaping those entrapments, intended to keep them in more or less unwitting slavery to the moronic aims of the tribal military-industrial complex.

"It goes without saying that certain definite skills and abilities not normally present in the life of ordinary man must be established if one hopes to become a permanent inhabitant of the Inner World.

"Of course, even without these essential skills one may visit the Higher Dimensions briefly.

"At first—and this is a Great Secret—one must make a model—an exact simulation—of one chamber in the Higher Dimensional sectors of the Great Labyrinth...as one conceives it presently. Then one is expected to wring the secrets out of it.

"One must live as if actually in the Higher Dimension, even though at first this is entirely imaginary.

"Fortunately, we have such a highly developed imagination that it will not be hard to imagine ourselves as already accepted as a native of the Higher Dimensions.

"Imagine yourself in a chamber about three meters square, just large enough to accommodate yourself somewhat comfortably without wasting space, and also one partner—or more—with whom you may wish to share this chamber—those to whom you would not mind being connected in the Higher Dimension for some time—perhaps forever.

"Then strive to know your human biological machine—in the sense of studying its habits, manifestations, gestures, expressions, thoughts and feelings completely, and study the biological machines of others with whom you intend to share your work chamber at least as completely as your own.

"For the moment, study of the deep essential selves of all possible chamber-mates is impossible, but study of patterns followed by the machine will provide some insight beyond the obvious mechanisms of simple primate behavior.

"Then we must try to know the deepest secrets of one another because, once built and occupied, this chamber, even though purely imaginary, cannot be easily dismantled," she concluded over a final burst of mortar fire coming in from the west.

"You don't expect me to believe one word of this wild bullshit, do you?" I asked in a mild tone.

"Let's try that thing again where we both take a powerdive into each other's heart," she suggested, pulling me gently by the sleeve toward an unoccupied alleyway.

Chapter Three

THE SHEMUTTI PLAIN

Our quest for artifacts brought us to Negub where we made some important finds, beginning with slabs of cuneiform cuttings, obviously the work of Assyrians.

Mesopotamia in the middle of March, brilliant Spring, the spirit of change washing over the face of the Nimrod Plain, the pastures of the *Jaif* luxuriating rich, luscious green.

Horses of the *Shemutti* and the *Jehesh* grazed on the greens surrounding the villages, the flatlands studded with the glistening white pavilions of the Hitta tribespeople, innumerable horses picketed at every stanchion.

Flowers of every hue and shade patinating the meadows with rich swatches of color, a patchwork quilt of clusters, Arab dogs stained from the blue, yellow and red flowers through which they'd been running.

The deserted village of *Naifa* swarmed with small wildlife—including every manner of strange vermin—as a result of which we were unable to sleep under the roof. We set our camp at the edge of a large pond which had filled a stone quarry on the outskirts of the village.

Salah, a young Arab woman with intense black eyes and short black hair—unusual for an Arab woman, even one not veiled in Purdah—helped to build the cookshack. She remained to help us and, when we returned in the evening, we spoke softly as the sun lay low on the horizon, visualizing what a sunset must have felt like many thousands of years ago here on the plains of Mesopotamia, at the very dawn of civilization.

The transparent veil of evening drew itself over the landscape, the distant ruin of *Keshaf* rising in the mist of twilight.

Struggling with the dying sun, the sounds of sheep and cattle flowing from the distant pastures, young girls bent to the task of milking, while the older girls and women returned from the river, gracefully bearing filled waterjugs on their heads, in a striding dance through the tall grass, like Masai plainswomen, their men passing on horses, tufts of ostrich feathers tipping their long spears, silhouetted darkly against the open sky.

One rider wheeled his horse around suddenly and rode up to our tent, reining up sharply as he drove the point of his lance into the ground. He sprang from his mount and coiled the halter to the shaft of the quivering weapon.

He sat hunched nearby us for some time, maybe sharing the still silence of the darkening plain, then at the rise of the moon, vaulted into the saddle and went as suddenly as he had arrived, his dark form vanishing in the gloom between the glittering fires nestled among the black Arab tents, the darkness and silence broken at odd intervals by the staccato barking of dogs.

There were dogs everywhere. Everybody had a dog, and there were plenty of dogs left over just in case someone didn't. My vivid imagination worked out a scenario for a time when humans no longer kept dogs as pets, when packs of dogs ran free as scavengers and predators.

Abd-ur-Rahim woke us one morning and, while Salah tried not to burn the pot as she boiled water and I tried equally intensely to crack an egg of some unknown species of what I hoped would have been a bird, offered to take us to what the Arabs called *Negub,* The Hole. The name wasn't very promising, and I had no idea what we'd be likely to see; probably just a hole in a rock, if I knew my Arabs.

Two hours later we reached the natural wonder. Sure enough, it was just another hole.

It bored its way through hardrock like a sideways pocket mine, then spilled out into a mile-long channel. Slabs of cuneiform cuttings had wedged themselves into a crevice. The entire place crawled with inscriptions.

From the looks of things, this was obviously the work of the Assyrians. The inscriptions must have been to commemorate the completion of the tunnel, whose purpose is somewhat uncertain. Perhaps it had been cut so that the waters of the Zab River could dump into the irrigation zone of the territory, or it may have been the spill coming out of the Great Canal, still visible as a double range of mounds near the ruins of the ancient city.

In spite of the uncertainty about specifics, we could see that the main slab contained an important inscription, a list of kings, probably unpublished. It wasn't worth our time to remove it carefully, but a few sticks of dynamite easily blew most of the tablet out of the rock, making quite saleable fragments.

This was an important find; without it we'd have had to wire for more money. The art dealers were very generous, which told me that my first instinct had been correct...it *had* been an important piece, of immense archaeological significance. It was just a shame we'd had to blow it apart, because it threw the list of kings out of sequence and most of the names were now virtually unreadable.

We managed to pry a head off one of the winged statues, promising ourselves that we'd come back for the remainder at some later date, and we would have, too, if we'd been able to remember exactly where we'd found it.

29.

Chapter Four

EXODUS

It's difficult to describe to a Westerner what it's like to be in the midst of a large tribe of desert Arabs in the process of migrating to new pastures....

About midday we found ourselves in the midst of immense herds of camels. Camels are not unique in the desert, of course, nor very hard to find. You could find a single camel blindfolded, and a herd of camels could be located entirely without sight, sound, touch, taste or temperature. All you really need to locate a camel is a nose. That's for an ordinary herd of camels. For an immense herd such as the one I'm describing, no nose is good news.

The resonant "whoop, whoop, whoop" of the *Haddidin* camelherders bounced back from the hills on all sides of us, as they galloped through the herd

on Appaloosa cutting horses, which they got who-
the-hell-knows-where.

Shortly after we rode up, I saw Mamoun barking
orders to several Arabs who obviously worked for
him on the digs and didn't know what to do since
there wasn't any sand to dig in at the moment. He'd
become quite rich by Arab standards, and looked
ripe for more.

We pitched our tents in the *Wadi Ghesub,* which
was formed by a salt stream forcing its way through
a dense marsh of reeds and water plants, from which
the valley takes its name.

About a dozen Arab tents were pitched around
ours, and Mamoun ordered a sheep slaughtered. As
much as I hate lamb's eyes over boiled rice, I hate
camel even worse, so I tried to be grateful for this
small blessing. We sat waiting in the Arab manner,
which is to say arrogantly, in true tribal macho style,
as the women prepared the large wooden bowls of
yoghurt. They unloaded a huge slab of fresh butter
at my place, which I resolved to eat only under
extreme duress. Butter always does something
strange to my intestinal tract, even when taken with
bread, and alone...the thought drove chills down my
backbone and brought on another small gut-
wrenching attack of the galloping willies.

The musky smoke of camel-dung fires filled my
lungs, curdled my nostrils and repelled any sense of
worldly values which might have remained, and the
shuffling forms of weak, decrepit old Arab
women...which means about thirty years old in that
part of the woods...kept the coals hot as the men
butchered the carcass and dumped the meat into the

boiling cauldrons. After an indeterminate time, during which the inevitable heated disputes erupted among the Arabs seated together around the fire, the meat was speared out of the kettles and dumped on huge wooden platters.

We ate with our fingers, the same as the Arabs, after which the servants ate, then the camel-drivers and tent crew, then finally, when every edible portion had been removed, it was more or less thrown to the women and dogs, not necessarily in that order. I had taken a serious risk in sharing my plate with Salah, but most of the men dismissed my action as that of a crazy American, and regarded both of us from that moment on as animals, something far beneath their dignity.

Mamoun offered to take us to a branch of the *Shamar* where he thought we might find some interesting antiquities. Up to this point, we had been more or less on a wandering course through the desert, but now we rode on a definite course toward the Tigris. Before nightfall we arrived at an Arab camp, the chief of which was Sheikh Khalaf.

Salah and I spread our carpets on the grass at a distance from the main group, and Mamoun's friend Ali joined us, passing a silver bowl filled with the deep fragrance of ruby-red wine, forbidden to the Moslems, but not to Ali, who was a Bektashi dervish. The Bektashi make a point of taking wine, to insure that no Moslems sit among them, and I certainly wasn't a Moslem. Salah was very Westernized; we would say today that she was liberated. Her short hair and lack of veil nearly cost her her life, but she accepted it as part of the necessity which drove her away from the mouse-like life of the Moslem woman.

It's difficult to describe to a Westerner what it's like to be in the midst of a large tribe of desert Arabs in the process of migrating to new pastures. The scene reminded me of the Red Sea crossing in the film, *The Ten Commandments:* mobs of people hauling carts, driving mares, dragging travois overloaded with bulging packages of precious belongings...swarms of humanity and animals moving across a once-quiet plain now ruffled and annoyed with the passage of thousands of feet scuffing the earth, making wounds in the clean soil, furrowing the high grass in a temporary cattle-path.

We soon found ourselves surrounded by enormous flocks of sheep, cattle and camels, and everywhere as far as the eye could see, people, people, and more people, aged and decrepit men and women, unable to walk, tied atop the heap of furniture and cookware, infants crammed into saddlebags, their tiny heads peeping out from the narrow opening, like newborns trying to decide whether or not to emerge from the womb.

The saddlebags containing children were balanced against lambs or kids tied on the opposite side. Young girls walked alongside the carts, draped in the clinging, contoured Arab shirt which emphasized their slim, graceful forms, to the total disinterest of the men. Now, if they had just a little more meat on their bones or had they been young *Circassian* boys...

Mothers carried children on their shoulders, their young sons driving flocks of lambs before them, horsemen riding to and fro across the plain, camel drivers urging their mounts with short hooked sticks and leading their highbred horses by their long halters, colts galloping everywhere among the teeming throng. We wended our way through this motley crowd for several hours, until we were able to stop a while and pitch tents.

Chapter Five

HOSPITALITY

We pitched our tents and went at once to the tent of the tribal chief. Rassam led the way to the head of the tent where we seated ourselves on very antique well-worn carpets and the ritual words of welcome began in earnest.

We had another two or three hours' ride before us, and by the time we reached our encampment, both we and our horses were exhausted by the heat of the sun and the day's wearing journey.

The tents were pitched on a broad lawn at the bottom of a deep, wide ravine. We went at once to a tent distinctively larger than the others of the approximately three-hundred Arabs who held dominion over the area. This was the tent of the tribal chief.

He was short and fat, his features regular and well-formed, but his expressive exuberance given to him by great nature and which had carried him through his youth was now hidden by a bloated, well-fed and pampered corpulence.

A heavy fringed yellow, red and blue striped kerchief with long braided cords was draped over his head and fell below the shoulders. A brightly colored band of grease-spattered silk-tied spun camel's wool held it in place above the brow. A black woolen *jalab* over a long white shirt which fell to his ankles completed his costume.

He and a man named Rassam or Rassim led the way to the head of the tent where we seated ourselves on very antique well-worn carpets, and when everyone in our party had found seats, the ritual words of welcome which had only been exchanged quickly before, now began in earnest.

"Peace be with you."

"May God protect you."

"Upon my head, you are welcome."

"My house is your house."

"Peace be with you, and may God be your protector."

This greeting was exchanged with each individual present, and while this vital half-hour ceremonial prelude to hospitality proceeded, I took the opportunity to appraise our hosts.

Nearest to me was Farhan, the chief's son, a handsome young man who was obviously intelligent, although his expression was neither agreeable nor attractive, and behind him sat his own personal followers, a crowd of ferocious and warlike creatures who had obviously spent the majority of their young lives exploring the subtleties of rapine and pillage and who regarded anyone not of their tribe as animals and therefore natural enemies to be killed or exploited or worse.

Greetings having been completed, conversation on general topics began in a wild fashion, and no discernible acknowledgement between conversants was anywhere in evidence.

Coffee, highly drugged with exotic desert roots, herbs and spices was served, which we were expected to consume before retiring to our own tents.

To nobody's surprise, the mixture was terribly aphrodisiac, and Salah and I greeted dawn after an unbearably erotic night. The usual Arab breakfast arrived, or what I had been led to believe was the usual breakfast endured by all Arabs everywhere...large wooden bowls and platters heaped with fragments of leftover boiled mutton swimming in melted butter and soured milk.

When the remains of our breakfast had been mercifully removed, we again met with the chief. At this time, he had only three wives on a continuing basis. His other wives had been married off to his attendants one by one.

For one reason or another, he had developed the habit of marrying a new wife every month, at the end of which he'd divorce her, perhaps out of partiality to the earliest stage of married life, the honeymoon.

The queen of his hareem, Amsha, was celebrated for her beauty and nobility. Her well-proportioned and graceful form was traced uncomfortably visibly through the thin linen gown.

She was very tall as Arabs go, and her dark brilliant eyes spun a web of fascination, set wide apart, contrasting with her fair skin and creamy complexion.

Enormous gold earrings dangled from her ears, terminating below the waist in carved and ornamented turquoise tablets. Great rows of heavy stone beads, Assyrian cylinder seals, coral and agate beads encircled her slender neck.

Gold rings jangled on her wrists and ankles as she walked. My eyes were riveted on her blue lips, indigo eyebrows connecting over the bridge of the nose, her forehead and cheeks splashed with darkened beauty marks, her black lashes heavy with kohl.

My vision wandered over her tattooed body, the flowered ends of which teased the eye, along her legs and the roundness of her breasts, the nose ring so large that it had to be removed in order for her to eat, talk or laugh, and finally came to rest on an exquisitely carved cylinder seal dangling about an inch and a half below her full, firm breasts.

My eyes remained rooted on the Assyrian cylinder seal for the rest of the evening, following its every movement until I could bear it no longer. I left the tent, resolving to continue excavations at *el-Hather*, where we'd found all those incredible cylinder seals, only this time, I intended to keep the best of them for my own collection.

When a desert tribe moves to new pasture, the women of the chiefs are placed on camels, but not just on ordinary saddles. They ride atop a giant butterfly, consisting of a light wooden framework over which is stretched a kind of parchment, in the center of which is a tiny pavilion, within which the women are encouched.

The entire contrivance is covered with glass beads, shells, string fringes and tassel ornamentation of every description.

As the camel sways across the desert, it gives the appearance of a gigantic sick, swollen butterfly staggering across the plain.

Chapter Six

ARAB LOVE LIFE

One of our two Arab guides interspersed his archaeological information with massive doses of spicy sexual ravings.

Al Hather lay about eighteen miles from the encampment, and two guides went with us to the ruins, one of whom talked reasonably coherently about antiquities, although he interspersed his archaeological information with massive doses of spicy sexual ravings.

"We Arabs think of only two things," he explained, "love and war. War—*Ya Bej*—everyone understands. What is there to understand about war? But nobody understands about love. Let us therefore speak of love, trying somehow to fathom its mystery."

He thereupon proceeded to dwell at length—
and in graphic detail—upon the more interesting
points about Arab women, and how much more
they were willing to offer to a man who has distinguished himself in combat.

"An Arab may fixate his affections quickly upon
any woman who has attracted his attention," he
droned on, "even as she passes him in the market or
bearing water from the well.

"Nothing can equal the intensity of this first wild
abandon. He flings himself at once into stupid and
desperate feats of strength and daring, balanced on
the one side by fierce optimistic desperation and on
the other by hopelessly deep melancholy."

"In America," I interjected, "we'd call that sort of
behavior paranoid manic-depressive."

"Naturally," he continued, as if I'd never made
the comment, "the woman to whom he has attached
himself is completely ignorant of this wild sentiment
she has inspired—of course only unconsciously and
devoid of interest of her own—and the lover then
makes serious efforts to make his passion known to
her.

"This is the point at which life for an Arab man
becomes exceedingly dangerous...

"He may at first try speaking to a relative or to
someone who has access to the hareem of the tent in
which she lives and, after binding his discretion by
a secret oath, beg his contact to arrange a meeting.

"If his confidant agrees to talk to the woman, he
confronts her when she is alone, and taking a flower
or a blade of grass, says to her, 'Swear by Him who

made this flower and who made us also that you will not reveal to anyone what I now tell to you.'

"She may or may not be interested in taking a lover, but if she refuses to honor the oath, the go-between simply goes his or her way and never discloses anything.

"Or she may take the oath, saying, 'I swear by Him who created this flower we now hold and who made the world which caused us to arise within it also,' and they settle on a time and place for the meeting.

"Vows of this sort are seldom betrayed, but when they are, the results are quite spectacular if you've never witnessed a public beheading before."

Chapter Seven

A MESOPOTAMIAN SOCK-HOP

The chief, having dismounted with exacting gravity, seated himself according to his own idea of his relative rank, which meant at the head of the table...

On our ride to Al Hather we passed enormous...what shall I call them?...flocks, I suppose, of Arabs crossing the plains with their families, livestock and tents, and everywhere the huge sick butterflies flapped, swayed and lurched unsteadily across the landscape.

Dark thunderheads rose ominously behind the ruins of Al Hather on our approach, although the rich golden-tinted limestone, for which the monuments of Syria are famous, still glinted like gold with the last rays of sunset.

We urged our mounts onward, trying at the last moment to evade the threatening storm, but its full fury burst down upon us long before we reached refuge.

The dancing electrical crackle of lightning threw brilliant washes of radiance on the ancient buildings, and thunder echoed through the time-worn halls. It was a beautiful moment, and we didn't want to spoil it by failing to take a souvenir.

I managed to pry several interesting figures off the palace wall, probably Sassanian, no earlier than the Arsacian dynasty, although the original buildings were a great deal older than that.

During our absence very little progress had been made on the excavation. The workers had moved some of the rubbish from the upper part of the chamber, and the lions had been almost completely uncovered. We knew we couldn't move them with the Land Rover. They were far too massive. But Ali soon solved that by sawing them into little blocks. You could hardly notice the cuts when they were put back together for sale, except that they were a few inches smaller in several directions.

Between the lions was a large pavement slab covered with cuneiform characters, but we had plenty of that sort of stuff, so we tore it up and stacked it in the corner.

In the course of clearing the entrance between the lions, we found numbers of copper ornaments, which we kept; inscribed alabaster tablets, which we also kept; and several dozen ducks or geese formed out of terra cotta, which I used for target practice, as I'd long since run out of clay ducks for my twelve-gauge.

The heads of the ducks—if that's what they were, and they certainly resembled ducks more than anything else except perhaps a jaybird—were turned, resting across the back, which was covered in some sort of undecipherable cuneiform characters, probably containing the name, title and genealogy of some king or other, if I know my Assyrians. We had found—and shot—similar objects in Egypt, but to me, a clay duck is a clay duck. Among the copper artifacts were a ram or bull which had evidently been carried in the mouth of the winged lion, several hands with fingers closed and slightly bent, which we were later able to sell as rather intriguing cigarette holders, and a few metal flowers, which we planted outside the tent.

The hands may have served as a casing for inscribed tablets, and the flowers for ornament. The purpose of the ducks I never have been able to adequately explain to myself, although I've lain awake nights wondering whether the ancient Assyrians had skeet shooting clubs.

Several locals had expressed interest in our discoveries, and before the summer's heat had set in and made the plain completely uninhabitable, I thought it might be politic to accommodate them.

Accordingly, we issued a general invitation to all the Arabs of the neighborhood, and several of the non-Moslem women were able to extract permission from their husbands to attend.

Borrowed white pavilions appeared on the broad, flower-carpeted lawn near the river. These were for the women and for the reception of the tribal chiefs.

Black tents had been provided by someone unknown for the guests, servers and one for the
kitchen. A few Arab warriors had been detailed to
oversee the horses, which had been picketed
anywhere there happened to be some available
space.

An open area had been left vacant between the
pavilions in case anybody wanted to dance during
the course of the evening, and for the exhibitions
which we had planned for the entertainment of the
general mob.

At the first gray of dawn, Abd-ur-Rahim rode up
on a tall roan mare, adorned with heaps of
embroidered finery. He wore a turban over his *kef-
fiah,* or kerchief. Fringes fell from the turban, mercifully concealing his neanderthal-like features.

He wore a long robe of red silk, underpinned by
bright yellow boots which he'd evidently removed
by force from some mortal enemy whose only crime
was owning those boots.

We'd hired some Kurdish musicians, and the
band arrived ready to play any selection we asked
for, so long as it was Arab.

The mock battle proceeding at the edge of camp
among the younger warriors of the tribe was almost
drowned out completely by the tooting and drum-
ming of the band, who for some unaccountable
reason felt it necessary to raise their efforts whenever some other sound seemed to threaten their total
audio domination of the territory. From that moment on until the end of the day, there was no
danger of silence for a single moment.

The chief, having dismounted with exacting gravity, with that peculiar fear of humiliation common to all tribal chiefs everywhere, seated himself according to his own idea of his relative rank, which meant at the head of the table, while his bodyguard picketed their mares in the usual way.

Slowly the other chiefs arrived and arranged themselves in a pecking order known only to themselves, while the common mob found places on the lawn.

A snack of sweetmeats, halvah, parched peas and lettuce salad, overabundant by any standard, had been prepared, along with fourteen sheep who had met their maker in honor of the occasion.

These had been roasted and boiled for the assembly, and brought out on large wooden platters which, after the men had thoroughly picked through it, were passed to the women and children.

After the final fragment had been devoured, the dancing began. The onlookers seated themselves in a large circle on the lawn, around the dance area, as the dancers formed a circle, holding hands and shuffling round, twisting the body in gyrations as they moved.

The music gained momentum, and as it did, the dancers quickened their pace, their movements becoming more and more active and vehement. The *debke* looks to the uninitiated Westerner something like Albanian folkdancing, but far more wild and extravagant.

When the dancers were exhausted, they collapsed on the ground. When the last dancer had wandered off, the warriors began the sword-dance.

As the excitement rose, several onlookers felt the necessity of relieving the dancers of their bladed weapons in favor of wooden staves, with which they whacked the hell out of one another, the crowd cheering them on at every successful contact.

The festivities lasted a full three days and nights, and made exactly the kind of impression I wanted to accomplish. After the first day, everyone forgot entirely about the artifacts, which we never did have to unpack for exhibit.

The heat of summer now began, and it became impossible to live under a white tent, while the vermin-infested huts were equally uninhabitable. We set up camp on the river, making a sort of bower of reeds and tree-boughs, forming a small semi-private chamber within which Salah and I were able to set up some form of housekeeping.

Scorpions and several nondescript reptiles of the smaller variety, of the species *Annoyus Eatusup,* soon found their way into our little apartment, followed by the charming local gnats and sandflies which ordinarily hovered over the river on any calm night when we didn't happen to be in the neighborhood; otherwise they all came to our house for supper, which was us.

The change to summer had been as sudden as the change to spring. The green plain perished in a single day, leaving brown burnt shrubbery, baked in the hot desert winds. Whatever vegetation had survived the ravages of that first heat was soon destroyed by dark flotillas of locusts, and in a few days, no trace of cultivation remained.

12

Chapter Eight

ONE WAY VOYAGE

Dry, dry, dry...very, very dry. What a hell-hole this part of the world was turning into, where even the water was dry.

Along about midafternoon that same day, Ahmed brought us by muleback to a wild ravine, thorns and thistles running round its perimeter like coils of barbed wire.

As it had every day, the sun bore down in a continuous stream of scorching radiation, drilling through every layer of clothing. We wore the native *jalab*, a hooded woolen robe, and linen underdress, but it didn't help much.

The oven-baked rocks and parched earth only served to make the heat more oppressive, turning the whole area into an enclosed crucible, the atmosphere almost unbreathable, forcing us to take short, open-mouthed, dog-like breaths.

Thoroughly panicked by my stifled breath, I searched wildly among my rapidly vanishing mercurial thoughts for some way to describe this experience, on the off-chance that we survived to tell the tale, but nothing came to mind except *hot, hot, hot...very, very hot.*

We scrambled up over the scorching rocks on the far slope, past tiny insects and far-off high-pitched sounds of some breed of desert creature, the nature of which escaped me then, and I'm no closer to a good guess now.

I had in mind an image of the Olympic torch-bearer, whose marathon seemed relaxed in comparison to the effort we were forced to make for every foot of ground on the broiling stones.

I groaned inwardly at the realization that we were going to have to descend this same oven on our return, and resolved if at all possible to arrange my affairs so that I'd never again have to go over the same ground on the return journey. From now on, if I had my way about it, every voyage would be strictly one-way.

For some unaccountable reason, my mind flashed back to an incident which occurred in New York City several years earlier and which had no apparent relation to the present circumstances.

On the upper west side of Broadway, I had discovered somehow a tiny cramped office, venetian blinds on the windows overlooking Broadway traffic, green and black linoleum edged with a rubbery plastic wall trim, eight-foot long fluorescent fixtures, a smell of commercial cleaners and roach spray.

On the far end—which wasn't all that far—stood a raised platform decorated with a tiny Tibetan monk, who typically sat very still and talked on and on for several hours each evening.

The thing that struck me about him was that he never seemed particularly interested in the people who showed up at his talks. Apart from that, I saw nothing unusual about him or his talks.

He'd get himself all cranked up on the subject of traditional Buddhism, suddenly sit up and say, "but that's all just bullshit," and then wander back through the door to the left of the platform, apparently finished for the night. One of his pupils would see us out and that would be that.

After several such nights, I asked a question, after which I was invited through the mysterious door. Until that evening, I had seen only the dull green and faded black chipped linoleum floor, soot-covered venetian blinds over the windows, bare platform and torn and greasy seat cushions with the stuffing poking out of them here and there, stacked up against the wall for the use of visitors.

The fluorescent lighting had always bothered me, but now I saw the flickering flames of candles—hundreds of candles—surrounded by a surprisingly enormous room. I realized that in back of the small front office there must have been a giant loft, which had been converted into what looked to me like all the Tibetan monasteries I had ever seen in photos.

We talked. I can hardly describe what we talked about, exactly, but as you'd expect, it had to do with the subject of rebirth.

What I'd asked him outside was if he'd ever thought about the idea that we were already in the Bardo, and that we weren't really awaiting death, but rebirth into the Real World...that basically this world was all a Bardo dream.

"What makes you think that?" he'd asked.

"It's all so plastic," I responded. "Things are too pat; everything fits too well to be the Real World. This universe is just too damn accommodating to be real."

"Too accommodating," he nodded. "That's what I think, too. And most of the monks I know agree with that view. We probably are in the Bardo right now. The instruction books are intended for the dead, you know. And that's us, isn't it?"

"I really don't know," I replied. "That's what I was hoping to find out from you. But if this is the Bardo, what's the Real World like? If the only world we know is just a Bardo dream, then what can we expect from the Real World?"

"It won't be like this," he thought he answered. Hell, it sounded to me like my stock market prophecies when I worked as a market analyst.*It'll fluctuate*, was my standard prediction...and I was almost always right.

Suddenly my thoughts snapped back to my body forcing itself upward along hot dry dirt...There, that was another word I could use to describe this experience. *Dry, dry, dry...very, very dry.*

At last we clambered over the edge onto a flat area which immediately ran downward into a still more tortuously twisting and turning ravine which ran along what looked like a dry river bed that probably hadn't had water in it since the days of Moses. *Dry, dry, dry...very, very dry.* What a hell-hole this part of the world was turning into, where even the water was dry.

Eventually we staggered and stumbled our way through the ravine, and found ourselves on what passes for a road anywhere outside California.

Now we had an entirely different problem. It would soon be dark, and we hadn't found a place to camp.

"Shit," our Arab guide muttered incongruously. I'd have thought he would snarl some exotic Arabic obscenity, but he didn't.

Chapter Nine

INSIDE THE TOMB

Nothing could withstand the fury of the sand and dust in the whirlwind which brought darkness for an hour, so we took refuge in the tomb. Returning to our riverbank we found no trace whatever of our dwellings.

The *Abu-Salman* tribe had transferred their people to *ozalis,* sheds constructed of reeds and long grasses, along the banks of the river.

The *Shemutti* and *Jihash* had returned to their villages, and the plain was as naked and desolate as it had been in the month of November.

Although the remaining number of workmen was small, the excavations were carried on as urgently—and as secretly—as possible. The lions had formed an entrance into a second chamber with sculpted walls which may originally have formed a facade.

The carved slabs had fallen good-side-downward on the chamber floor, which was dry, which may have been why they were so unusually well-preserved.

Once again faced with the problem of raising the multi-ton stones in a closed and compressed chamber, we were forced to come to the opinion that dynamite was obviously out of the question; otherwise we'd have used it.

While we were debating in the underground chamber, a violent whirlwind swept over the plains, bringing darkness for an hour. Nothing could withstand the fury of the sand and dust, and returning at once to our riverbank we found no trace whatever of our dwellings.

The tent had vanished completely, and the tattered remains of my surplus camping furniture, such as it had been, were scattered for thousands of meters.

Our only refuge was the tomb itself, and Salah and I tried to find something useful to do underneath the lions, while we waited for the storm to spend the major force of its fury.

This type of storm is typical of Mesopotamia, Babylonia and Susiana during the early part of the summer, and the fury, violence and dense darkness are difficult to convey to someone who has never been in one. After the storm had passed, we settled the problem of quartering the large stone slabs with a saw of the type used in quarries.

People always like heads and faces, and dealers typically don't want to buy whole figures unless they're small enough to stick in the front window, so we could see at a glance how to approach this.

On the second slab we managed to chip away the stone around a head of a king who had been holding a bow in one hand and two arrows in the other. He was followed by a eunuch who bore a mace, backup bow and a quiver of arrows, just in case he missed with the first two and broke the bow, obviously a serious consideration of the period.

A vizier stood facing him followed by another eunuch. I assume it was a eunuch. Kings were partial to eunuchs, always have been, probably always will be, so when you see an Assyrian or Babylonian king followed by a fat pampered creature somewhat humanoid in form, you can make a safe bar-bet; it'll be a eunuch.

Chapter Ten

OBJECTIVE ARCHAEOLOGY

One thing about an antiquity; it has to be believable, and everyone knows that old things just don't survive intact. So we made sure to distress our finds accordingly....

The first slab was richly and elaborately carved. We cut off chunks that contained bracelets, armbands and weapons adorned with ram and bull heads, and, when we got them down to the river, washed off the color remaining on the hair, beards and sandals, knowing that the dealers would be suspicious of anything that looked too good or too clean or that wasn't broken.

I'd learned this by watching one Cairo dealer smash a large Eighteenth Dynasty limestone relief on the pavement outside his shop. Just looked too good, that's all. One thing about an antiquity; it has to be believable, and everybody knows that old things just don't survive intact.

Luckily, the larger slab had already been broken into several smaller fragments, but the lower section remained in place. After a number of utterly unsuccessful attempts to carve it up, we decided to leave most of the bottom part, which presently resides in the state museum, with the exception of the faces and hands which form the major part of several private collections including my own.

There was another, extremely massive slab with a heroic carving in relief of a winged figure with a three-horned cap, bearing a fir cone and some sort of square thing. It looked very similar to several others we'd already found, and since even the head was far too large to load into the Land Rover, we settled for a very expressive and marketable forefinger and a beautifully sandaled right foot.

In carrying one of the larger slabs out of the chamber, one of the lions happened to fall. We rescued the head...of course...and underneath it, stumbled onto a half-buried cache of sixteen copper lions in descending sizes from about twelve inches in length to a little over an inch.

Because of the rings cast on their backs, I assumed these were weights of some sort. I brought back several of the smaller creatures, the largest of which is presently a paperweight on my desk; the smaller weights would have made marvellous keyrings if they hadn't all worn clean down to shapeless metal blobs except for this last one that I carry like the others, in my right-hand pocket.

One of the unfortunate things about archaeology is that archaeologists keep coming along and taking everything away before serious collectors can excavate them properly.

A partly broken terra-cotta vase leaned in a corner; it was embellished with two winged and taloned priapus-like figures, each breasted like a human woman, with the tail of a scorpion.

We were after gold and gemstones, so normally, I wouldn't have bothered to collect the fragments, but I knew several gay dealers in New York would pay anything for ancient terra cotta just so the figures were male, human and well-endowed. Accordingly, I carefully packed the fragments for shipping.

From the second slab, which had shown the siege of the city, we managed to separate chunks with part of the battering ram and the rolling tower.

The third slab contained a low relief carving of a lion hunt which, from the view of composition and effective art, the spirit of the grouping and its extraordinary state of preservation, would probably have been the finest and most profound specimen of Assyrian art in existence if we hadn't mislabeled it in the dock lading and shipping instructions.

It may well grace somebody's flagstone garden walkway in La Jolla, California, for all I know. I just hope it didn't end up in a Salvation Army store, that's all.

About the time we'd removed the aforementioned artifacts, we had word that government troops were in the area, which made extensive excavations impossible. Within the hour, we had trace-lessly vacated the premises.

I determined to open trenches near Mosul but not so close that we were in danger of running afoul of the authorities.

Actually, the only opposition we received was from a French team who tried to claim the ruins as French property *vis-à-vis* the Napoleonic wars. Well, they dug on their side of the mound, and we dug on ours.

As we punched our way through the overbur-den, a few rag-tag fragments of sculpture turned up, the inscriptions of which were so legible we were obliged to sandblast them into unreadability.

Subsequent excavations disclosed a chamber at the base of the north side of the mound. Entrance was gained by blasting apart an elaborately carved multi-ton alabaster slab about eight feet by ten feet, about two feet thick. Behind it we saw descending steps, revealing a chamber with a raised sacrificial altar, evidenced by an alabaster slab with conduits for blood runoff.

Underneath the altar, which we finally moved with the assistance of large crowbars and comealong winches, we found a large cache of gold leaf and repoussé.

Behind the altar was a slab about eight feet high, portraying a king on a throne. We had plenty of kings on thrones, however, so we didn't bother to slice it up as we had the others.

Chapter Eleven

THE FRENCH EXCAVATIONS

I knew that security tended to be very poor, and thought it would be relatively easy to buy some of the more interesting excavated goods from the workmen at Khorsabad.

On the twenty-eighth of August, preparations for our departure to the Tiyari mountains had been completed and that was the day, according to my diary, that we left the city of Mosul on horseback, with *Buyuruldis*—government papers—as far as Amadiyah, and a letter for the *Berwari* chief, through whose territory we intended to pass.

I also had a letter of introduction to the *meleks* and priests of the Nestorians.

We were anxious to see how the French excavations were getting along at Khorsabad, because I knew that security tended to be very poor, and thought it would be relatively easy to buy some of the more interesting excavated goods from their workmen, so we made Khorsabad one definite stopping place on our way to the mountains.

The twenty-eighth was particularly hot and dusty. It was the sixth day of Ramadan, and the Moslems were still sleeping off their hunger as we passed through the city gates and crossed the boat-bridge. We arrived at Khorsabad in about two and a half hours' ride.

There had been a village perched on the mound, but the French had long ago purchased the buildings, moved the locals out, and developed excavations.

The Khausser, a small river—or perhaps the word is riverlet—branches out from the Makloub foothills, and is used to irrigate the rice fields. The marshy ground breeds ill health, and several of the French workmen had developed fevers, and consequently were too sick to work at the excavations.

Having missed several days of work, they naturally hadn't been paid, which was the French policy, and we found it very easy to persuade them to sell us some of the better pieces that had been found, including some rather spectacular lapis figurines and gold crowns of leaves and grapes, similar to Attic Greek pieces of the period.

We had learned to pay our workmen whether they worked or not, and often actually bought pieces from them to prevent them from bringing them to dealers themselves.

Chapter Twelve

In the
Sarmoung District

**For centuries the Yezidi were a powerful tribe
in the Sarmoung District, but terrorism on the part
of the Christians and Moslems alike forced them to
gradually cloak their teachings in secrecy.**

Khorsabad, the gateway to the Yezidi District, is
a town which occupies the site of the ancient
Assyrian city Sarmoun. This ancient city was mentioned by Arab geographers, and Yakuti mentions in
his *Annals of the Arab Conquests* that Sarmoun, which
had been the site of an ancient temple, was a source
of considerable Assyrian treasure.

In the late Eighteenth Century, excavations
were carried on by Botta in the hopes of discovering
further treasures, and many journalistic reports of

these excavations still exist, mostly in Russian and Armenian periodicals of the period.

We had a few hours to conduct a cursory examination of the ruins of Sarmoun, which showed an already well-developed attack several years before. I had little hope of finding anything here, and we pressed on through the marshlands.

We passed the night surrounded by stagnant water and the gnats which infested them. I just hoped that there would be something left after they got through with us, at least enough to scrawl down a traveler's warning explaining that we'd been devoured by little tiny gnats.

The next morning we made a small ride and reached the springs of the Khausser at the northern side of the Jebel Makloub which courses past Mosul on its way into the Tigris near Kouyunjik.

We rode on into the Kurdish foothills. The plain was parched and barren, the heat intense as usual, the ruins of modern villages marked by mudbrick walls. Kurds rode past with loads of grapes for the market below.

By late afternoon, we arrived at the Yezidi village of Ain Sifni. We'd seen the brilliant white of its houses and conical tombs for several hours, and its clean-ness was a relief after the unbearable filth of the Moslem and Christian habitations.

We rode on two more hours through a mild pleasant valley enriched by a mountain torrent rushing past great clusters of flowering oleanders. At dusk we arrived at a wooded basin from the center of which rose the glistening white spire of the most central of all Yezidi shrines, the tomb of Sheikh Adi.

We were soon ensconced in a grassy knoll under the protective shade of a knot of lofty trees. The sudden switch from heat, salty sweat, dust and swarms of bugs to the sweet and verdant springs of this Yezidi retreat produced an immediate result; we passed the night in dreamless sleep somewhere in the vicinity of total oblivion, the fountain lulling us into a conviction of our complete safety.

We flung ourselves onto the lawn under the trees, and knew nothing until the first light of dawn, when we rose, broke our fast with a light breakfast of tea and rice-cakes, and wandered on foot into the wooded valleys surrounding the tomb.

The Yezidis had been a very powerful tribe some years back, and the Sarmoung District was their principal stronghold, more or less extending outward from the Jebel Sinjhar, a solitary mountain rising out of the Mesopotamian desert north of Mosul.

The last known independent chief of the Yezidi was Ali Bey, father of Hussein. He fought the Kurds for years until he was captured by the Ruwandis and executed.

He had fled with the villagers of Sheikhan to Mosul. It was spring and the river had overflowed its banks, so the boat bridge had been removed.

A vast mob of women and children remained on the banks and were overrun by the troops of Ruwandis Bey, who began an indiscriminate slaughter of Yezidis.

Moslems living in Mosul witnessed this wholesale murder in silence. They were happy enough to be rid of a troublesome and strange sect.

The population of the Sinjhar were massacred several times by Moslems, reducing the Yezidi tribe to one-fourth of its previous population.

The Yezidis took refuge in caves, within which they were suffocated by fires lit at the mouths, or destroyed by explosive charges or point-blank cannon fire.

The Yezidi had for years been victimized by the Moslems. The Turkish hareems had been recruited from them, and when the mercenaries of the Pashas of Baghdad were in pay arrears, they were turned loose on the Yezidi as an easy way of satisfying their demands.

This practice was responsible for atrocities that make the Nazis look like pussycats, and it wasn't unnatural or unexpected that the Yezidi should organize themselves into resistance groups.

This was just the excuse that the Pashas needed for an open invasion of the Sinjhar. As a result, the Yezidi were almost completely annihilated, and the few who remained alive clung ferociously to their religion in the face of death by torture.

Many people who openly profess Islam are actually Yezidi, and maintain secret lines of communication with the Yezidi priests.

During the last of the great massacres, Hussein had been carried off by his mother into the mountains, where he was brought up by the Yezidi priests and from his infancy had been regarded by them as their chief.

It was against this background of terrorism committed by the Christians and Moslems that the Yezidi began to cloak their teachings in secrecy.

Many people have reported that the Yezidi priests, particularly the chief priest, seem to know nothing about the Yezidi teachings.

This is easy to understand in light of the fact that the chief priest was usually the first to be put to death during the reign of terror under the Pashas of Baghdad.

After several hundred chiefs had been slaughtered, endangering their oral tradition and leadership, the Yezidi hit upon a plan; substitutes for the chiefs were chosen from among the most expendable members of the tribe. They were treated as chiefs and priests in the presence of strangers, and of course, not being real priests and chiefs, they knew nothing of religious matters and were totally unable to explain their ideas, which is a common complaint of visitors to the Yezidi.

This protective strategy is still carried on. The Pashas no longer exist, but Moslems are encouraged to betray non-Moslems, and the Yezidi are convinced that the massacres will occur again and, considering everything I know about Christian crimes in the name of Christ and Moslem crimes in the name of righteousness, I can't say I blame them for being suspicious, even after several decades of relative peace.

Very few researchers have ever penetrated the secrets of the Yezidi. To understand the Moslems' view of the Yezidi, it is necessary to remember that Moslems make a definite distinction between believers and nonbelievers, treating nonbelievers in much the same way that all human tribes everywhere do, which is to say, one's own tribe is composed of "the people" and all other tribes are animals, not quite human, and therefore fair game.

When it comes to dealing with non-Moslems, no treaty or oath is binding, and they may be attacked, killed, cheated or destroyed without mercy.

16

Chapter Thirteen

VISIONS IN THE STONE

I walked into the tomb and received a series of definite instructions which formed the basis for my eventual understanding of psychic emotional recordings as a technique for encapsulating esoteric information.

On our second day among the Yezidi, we visited a very old cemetery reputed to contain the crypts of ancient priests; at the moment this seemed like a brilliant idea.

And the reason it seemed so brilliant was that I was on the tail end of my first and only major experiment with alkanes—in this case, Polish Vodka—and found myself thoroughly unable to move a muscle except to roll over and vomit.

My companions managed to haul me to the cemetery and lay me on the wet grass. They heaved the enormous stone lid just sufficiently to load my inert form into the crypt.

At first nothing happened. I thought that I had fallen asleep when I began to see images of people as if a cinema were unravelling rapidly before my eyes.

Having not yet made extensive experiments with seances and psychic readings using hypnagogic trance, and seances with no trance at all, I had in myself no data for this experience other than pure speculation.

After a while I opened my eyes and sat up, eventually coming to grips with my situation. *If I'm alive, why am I in a crypt?* I wondered. *...and if I'm dead, why do I have to go to the bathroom?*

I decided after this experience to visit several museums of ancient art, with the idea that if one crypt contained images which transmitted themselves to an attentive observer, other artifacts might also exist.

I began to theorize that this phenomenon must be associated in some way with strong emotion, perhaps felt by thousands participating in a ritual, or suffering in combat.

In one museum a large part of an ancient Egyptian tomb had been reassembled. Arousing in myself the same general mood I would place myself in for a seance or a psychic reading, I walked into the tomb and received not just any set of images but a series of definite instructions which formed the basis for my eventual understanding of psychic emotional recordings as a technique for encapsulating esoteric information for future generations without the need to resort to the intentional formation of religions for the preservation of work ideas in general.

I was gratified to discover that it was easily possible to hear some sounds and to also receive definite sensations, most of them in the emotional centrum but some in the moving centrum and some in the instinctive centrum, which corresponded to the scenes viewed by me in the semi-trance state I had partly induced and which was partly induced by the suggestion of the artifacts surrounding my organic self.

My experiment came to an abrupt end when I was rather forcefully asked to quit the premises; my motionless presence had apparently upset other visitors to the gallery.

I was interested to note that the removal and reassembly of the tomb had no obvious deleterious effect on the thought-tapes, although I was not able to measure the difference between its original emanations and the emanations it transmitted in the new installation.

In another museum I began to receive not images but purely emotional readings; a choreographed series of atmospheric ambience which seemed to repeat itself endlessly.

After these experiences I formulated the idea that living images and sometimes real data recorded in times more ancient than those known by contemporary human primates—where individuals had advanced their civilization far beyond that of the present in every conceivable way other than technologically—could be obtained through the process of intentionally unlocking certain artifacts, some recorded deliberately by ancient esoteric societies and some accidentally by emotional upheaval or shock.

I began actively for the first time to seek direct ancient historical data and to compare it to archaeological and socio-anthropological reconstructions of ancient times as viewed by contemporary human primates.

I could not bring myself to believe that all the information held by contemporary man about the ancient world was totally and completely wrong.

I began to realize that the data collected from these artifacts could be used to formulate a whole new view of history.

Along with this I was able to examine some elements of future history also.

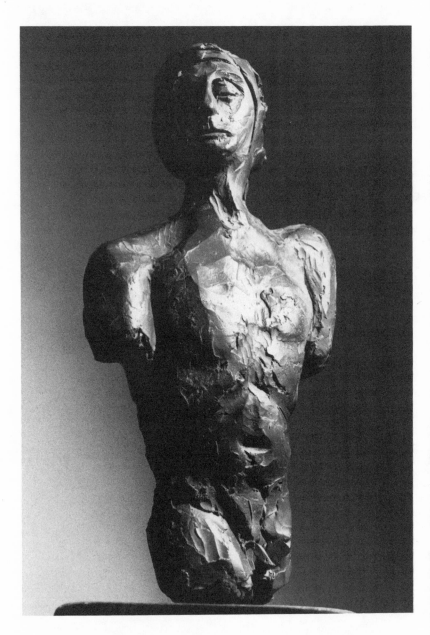

E.J. Gold, *The Medici Jester*, Bronze,
10-3/4", Edition of 22, 1988.

Chapter Fourteen

PLACES OF INITIATION

Special emotional states are part of the "Science of Keys" used to "open" artifacts in order to receive knowledge, attain gradations of initiation, and pass through unknown and forbidden sectors of the Great Labyrinth.

In my work with archaeological artifacts, I found that in many of them some images and a definite ambient atmosphere had been induced, probably in much the same way that a wire can be magnetically influenced to contain thought and emotional patterns of speech or music, and concepts can be recorded electromagnetically on a magnetic disk or volatile memory cartridge.

Almost every intentionally recorded artifact made during or after the Achaemenid Empire can be triggered using a single definite and intense emotional state, if emanated from a fully operational emotional centrum.

Many such artifacts have over the centuries ceased to have meaning, and since their real significance has been lost, they have more or less become the inner cores of religious or healing shrines.

The majority of these are now impossible to penetrate, not that it would do the average Western investigator any good, without the necessary psycho-emotional state of "organic mortification" and "emotion-of-humiliation" in addition to the mood of "hope-and-prayers-not-for-oneself-or-humanity."

Such special emotional states are part of the "Science of Keys" used to "open" artifacts in order to receive knowledge, attain gradations of initiation, and pass through unknown and forbidden sectors of the Great Labyrinth.

Artifacts of the reading variety are made even today by certain esoteric groups who, by one means or another, arrange to place them within temples and shrines.

Thus, initiation is instantly available as these artifacts are unlocked through the intentional or accidental proximity of someone in one of these unusual emotional states.

In this way, an individual on the path may pass knowingly or unknowingly from one place of initiation to another, but not entirely automatically, since each new initiation becomes accessible only after previous knowledge has been used in a practical way and therefore transformed into some form of understanding.

In addition, the process of transmission is accessible only to someone *who has necessity,* which is to say, someone whose path already leads in the direction of a place in the Work.

In this sense initiation is strictly from the self and cannot be conferred by another, because it is an emotional key, not in the negative spectrum, which unlocks the knowledge contained in the artifact, not merely information or technique.

As this occurs, the inner parts of the human biological machine are unlocked down to the deepest psychological and emotional levels, but without an artifact this would be completely useless.

Often even a small part missing from the whole will render an artifact inoperable. In still other cases the original transmission is missing, but a wave of higher emotion can still be detected by the higher emotional centrum, such as that evoked by the Great Pyramid, an ancient astronomical observatory adopted by the Pharaoh Khufu as his personal tomb.

In modern esoteric societies, we are only likely to encounter automatic psychics, emotionally overcharged people who are able to infuse amulets with power for protection and health, or make love charms, which is to say, an attractive emotional force contained electromagnetically in a small object, in much the same way that a needle can be magnetized by stroking with a magnet...hopefully for the good.

Using the *Law of Resonance,* two similarly pitched tuning forks can be made to resonate together, the struck tuning fork influencing the unstruck tuning fork to vibrate in sympathy.

In the same way, a new artifact—if constructed in the exact proportion, color and atmospheric ambience of the original—can be made to function exactly as the ancient or other-dimensional artifact, which is for one reason or another not available.

We have ways of knowing what some now-extinct artifacts looked like, and with knowledge of very simple skills such as plaster casting and miniature modeling, we can make a very effective copy which will function in the same way.

It became obvious to me that artifacts could be manufactured in resonance with artifacts even in other cosmoses, galaxies, dimensions...even in an ordinarily inaccessible part of the spectrum of reality far beyond our perception and comprehension.

All reading artifacts function in more or less the same way, but the Universal Key—and there is a Universal Key—must first be obtained. This is not a new science; it existed long before us, and will be here long after we are gone.

I found to my complete shock that it was as easy to learn these things as it would be to learn any science which is also an art. Only a long, serious study of human primates revealed why this obvious fact has remained unknown throughout human history.

E.J. Gold, *Shadow Under the Wall,*
Acrylic on canvas, 20" x 24", 1987.

Chapter Fifteen

FAITH

Finding myself momentarily outside the domain of human primate perceptions, I was able to view the entire sequence of events on a planetary basis for the whole of organic life.

The function of necessity must be an important factor; I had seen that faith—real faith, the kind of faith that tells you that everything is going to happen as it should as long as the effort goes into it—could transform one from receiving to supplying force-for-work.

Real faith is not a permanently fixated comfortable belief in something someone told you. It's knowing with the whole of your being that whatever is really necessary will appear when it's needed, and not a moment before....

This intelligent use of the impulse "faith" is the dividing factor between a group which studies ideas and a group which is working with ideas in a practical way.

Is it useful, I wondered, to arrange events for ourselves intentionally so that our attention is forced to divide itself into two or more mutually-denying tasks?

Thinking along these lines, while absorbing a seared steak kabab at my favorite cafe, I happened to conspire to overhear someone speaking at the table next to mine....

Just then, before he was able to complete his sentence, someone at the next table also began to speak about something seemingly entirely unrelated.

But as I heard these two statements woven together by synchronicity, taking these supposedly unrelated fragments as one connected idea coming from a single source-of-all-thoughts, I began to think in very different categories than human primate.

When I was able to blend seemingly fragmented separate parts into a whole connected idea which was being expressed through several conversations, I felt somehow closer to real ideas and to their primary source....

I concluded from this that if we were able to see and hear correctly, all events and phenomena would unfold in their objective sequence and not the usual subjective, making us immediately aware of the higher cosmic source of all ideas of the organic, emotional and thought.

It became obvious at a glance that if we were able to voluntarily connect the emotional emanations from Above we could see and understand the emotional whole mood in the same way that we ought to be able to see and understand events in their mental connotations.

Finding myself momentarily outside the domain of human primate perceptions, I was able to view the entire sequence of events on a planetary basis for the whole of organic life and in particular for man, including the whole of all planetary vibrations which, unfortunately, I have since more or less completely forgotten but, by God, for a moment there, it suddenly all made sense....

During the meat course, I felt the combined result of planetary vibrations more in terms of waves than of exact ideas, and by dessert, I was already aware of exact ideas directed downward into the lower dimensions from Above.

It was interesting to note the texture of the *blanc mange* pudding and at the same time continually sense the radiations feeding all organic life on Earth and the resulting emanations returning from them in the same way that a cockroach resists radium.

E.J. Gold, *I am Sad to See You Still on Earth*,
Acrylic on Canvas, 36" x 48", 1987.

Chapter Sixteen

ARTIFACT PSYCHOMETRIZING

The man of will is able to voluntarily arouse emotions for the opening of artifacts. Every important esoteric artifact has its own obscure, humorous or absurd key, some quite ingenious in their originality.

Will is the voluntary part of the thinking centrum; ordinary man has no voluntary part of the thinking centrum—all his thinking, particularly that part of thinking which could direct his moving centrum, is involuntary-passive-association-by-similarity.

What makes a good objective scientist?

The non-expectant. To be impartial to data and to have no "ax-to-grind." A real scientist does not see a paradox when two opposite ideas seem to prove themselves true. He realizes that he does not have the complete data.

When we see the whole picture we realize that the left-hand monkey wrench and the right-hand monkey wrench are two sides of the same coin.

If we can be impartial to data we can use the big key to artifact psychometrizing—emotion.

In general, emotion of this type and scale does not "just happen"; it must be voluntarily aroused. The emotion of "voluntary hysteria" for instance is very different from its involuntary cousin. Involuntary hysteria does not open any artifact of any real consequence, although it may attract the attention of certain infernal entities....

Another common emotional key for the opening of artifacts is "voluntary delirium," a variation of which is "voluntary ecstasy," both of which were very popular with the Babylonian tribes for their artifact recordings.

The man of will is able to arouse these emotions easily. For ordinary organic man it is utterly impossible.

The idea of "contamination" is very important when using emotional keys to unlock artifacts.

Lower, involuntary emotions must not be mixed with voluntary emotion; even a small momentary contamination of the two types of emotional arousings can destroy the vibration of the key for a very long time, perhaps even forever.

Not every emotion, whether higher or even saintly, is *apropos* to an artifact. Every artifact has its own key, some quite ingenious in their originality.

Many emotional keys are very difficult to arouse and are not common in the life of ordinary man at all.

The Dance of 100 Steps must also be some kind of artifact, in fact, a series of one hundred artifacts gathered from all parts of the Great Cosmos, each one of which requires a different exact emotional and psychological key for release of special data and transforming factors.

Each exact posture has the possible moving centrum data making possible the transference of data and transforming factors by means of receptivity to the exactitude of the posture.

Each posture represents an invented posture for the Absolute resulting from the practice of Sacred Objective Prayer.

E.J. Gold, *The Dress Rehearsal,*
Acrylic on canvas, 24" x 36", 1986.

Chapter Seventeen

THE ANCIENT SCIENCE
OF LEGOMINISM

In relation to each other some recordings indicated the existence of a "Master Plan" of the Work in which the locations of centrums of work-force, planetary networks of connecting force, and the whole plan for the evolution of the Inner Circle of Humanity were given.

Several esoteric societies through the ages have claimed to have discovered the psychometric secrets of the artifact—"Soorptkalknian Thought-Tapes" intentionally recorded in the mineral-kingdom-bodies of various ancient artifacts.

I found in my own investigations that they had simply gathered fragmentary data in the same way that contemporary spiritualist mediums experiment in contacts with various entities—that is to say, "willy-nilly."

This was unfortunately for my personal peace of mind true also of the contemporary esoteric society upon which I had begun earlier to rely as a source of authentic ancient data.

Soorptkalknian Thought-Tapes had for many years been attributed to contemporary initiates in the Himalayas as the "telepathic-source-of-data", involuntarily perpetuating the myth that artifact transmission of data is not ancient.

On the other hand, one cannot talk back to these recordings, nor ask questions. One can only watch and listen. The data on how to implant these thought-tapes is embedded in some of the recordings.

What we do in relation to artifacts is not unique. If it were, there would be today no surviving ancient knowledge, for *contemporary man has no basis whatever for legominism*—transmission of Great Ideas through art, architecture, dance, drama, music, and so on.

The only possible source for ancient data is now, and has been for many centuries, the recordings of data contained in artifacts released by emotional and psychological keys, voluntarily or involuntarily, by the great world-teachers.

Since there are many teachers all with the same exact doctrine, there must have been many who did the same as we with artifacts, although not necessarily in exactly the same way.

The question is, how complete was their data? How large a view were they able to take?

We must also question whether they were able to grasp the significance of these fragments of unknown doctrines.

Obviously if the doctrine is not complete, it is next to useless and very dangerous. The entire doctrine must be found if it is to be actively employed in personal evolution for the sake of the Work....

One must be able to find all necessary data; for this, one must be able to obtain a map which shows the location of all important artifacts embedded with thought tapes during the height of the ancient knowledge....

There are many maps of ancient monuments; before embarking on any expedition we must know as fully as possible the reliability of such maps.

All modern societies, both esoteric and ordinary, disappointed me; they did not have authentic maps. Most esoteric societies had not obtained the whole doctrine...*but they were content to remain partly ignorant.*

Their lack of concern for those depending upon their data made me, for the first time in many years, genuinely angry. I resolved to locate and make accessible the whole data of the Work for those innocents who were duped by the auspicious externals and suspicious internals of these contemporary "initiates of new formation."

My personal elucidations demonstrated that in general each artifact intentionally constructed for the encapsulation of Soorptkalknian Thought-Tapes had been exactly made according to strict mathematical rules of proportion relative to the compass, keeping in mind that planet Earth has shifted at least twice on its axis, which must be compensated for in our calculations.

Early alchemical data for the amalgamation of base and noble metals into what contemporary man calls "alloys" gave me the basis for more data on ancient monuments.

Finally in an auction house I was able to obtain the first edition of the Vesalius treatise on anatomy published in 1543, containing illustrations pointing to the exact locations of various early school monuments, within which certain very ancient artifacts had been embedded by their artisans under direct school commission.

Most Western occultism reposed in the hands of secret school communities at that time, and most of the members were respected members of ordinary society, primarily doctors and other scientific investigators. This of course was in a day when physicians worked in an atmosphere of personal scientific inquiry. Today they are largely content to leave research in the hands of graduate students and pharmaceutical companies.

Some recordings when taken in relation to each other began to indicate the existence of a "Master Plan" of the Work in which the locations of centrums of work-force, planetary networks of magnetic lines of connecting force, and the whole plan for the evolution of the Inner Circle of Humanity were given.

Nostradamus also discovered this whole body of work-data. In it the entire history of humanity in elaborate detail, from its beginnings with the introduction of the species to the planet to its very end in a Great Conflagration, is recorded.

At the same time all the possible transformations of the self and the keys for their activation—the entities from whom these can be extracted for a price—are given.

From these "Master Plan" artifacts I deduced that all authentic monuments are connected and come to us from the same original source in Sumeria.

We cannot open artifacts if we have any personal radiations between ourselves and the artifact. If we are busy emitting our personal recordings, we only allow those impressions pleasing to our present views—in the subjective.

Ordinarily, organic man lives "just-so", striving for perpetual personal comfort. Transmission of Soorptkalknian Thought-Tapes is not for him; he cannot take a new idea outside the scope of his ordinary comfortable ideas.

For receptivity to thought tapes we must have already created in ourselves a vacuum somehow in which we have a real necessity for data and transformation.

In order to obtain verification for all this I began to form a fellowship for the investigation of artifact phenomena.

From the idea that I could get nothing just for myself, but a group necessity would make possible the obtaining of at least data, I was able to get help from Above. They would perhaps take pity not on me, but on those depending on me for authentic data, making accessible the necessary corresponding data for work on self.

Almost certainly everyone who is in a school comes into contact with many real artifacts at one time or another in their lives or they would not present themselves to be prepared for the Work.

Some artifacts have *influence* on us for work, and for those who already have the beginnings of a magnetic centrum, they have great force of influence.

To evoke a corresponding emotional key in ourselves when in the presence of an artifact, and to at the same time prepare ourselves with real necessity for data and transformation, is one way in which we can be *able to do.*

We may know and even understand that we ought to evoke in our common presence certain blendings of emotion, thought and activity during Sacred Prayer, but if we have not had practice for a long time beforehand, we may not, even though we know exactly which thoughts, activities and emotions to evoke, be able to voluntarily perform this on the organic part of our selves.

To psychometrically penetrate an artifact may take some time; maybe several visits. It may be necessary to read it several times or even several hundred times before its meaning, even in the superficial ordinary sense, can be fathomed, and then to understand it as a whole can be the work of many years.

E.J. Gold, Blaue Reiter, Bronze,
16-1/2", Edition of 22, 1988.

Chapter Eighteen

THE NECESSITY FOR DATA

It took years to obtain data, and many more before that just to get data to be able to get data. I had the basis for the search; those who come after me have the basis for continuation and initiation of future generations of workers in the Work.

Since the method of Soorptkalknian Thought-Tapes was developed in relation to mineral artifacts, the techniques of "Legominism" are no longer necessary.

First came the method of recording data and sometimes even real knowledge in dance, music, art, architecture and crafts, such as carpet manufacture.

Then came the method of recording data directly in artifacts of stone, bronze, and so forth. Originally only organic objects of the animal and plant kingdom could be implanted, but later it became possible to use mineral kingdom artifacts, making longer survival possible.

Most contemporary esoteric and mesoteric societies have only limited access to artifacts for many ordinary reasons: attitudes, beliefs, prejudices, superstitions and perversions of the contemporary custodians of the said artifacts.

Some artifacts are accessible only to those with *developed powers....*

Others can be carried in a pocket. Not all artifacts are monumental.

I still have in my possession somewhere or other a small artifact from Greece from which I was able to view the exact formulation for special oracular vapors from the Oracle at Delphi, along with an ancient science of spices, herb lore, poisons and "assisting factors" for foods.

Also in another small artifact which was at one time part of a larger monument can be found an early formulation of the Periodic Table of Chemical Elements arranged in octaves.

It took me many years to obtain this data, and many more before that just to get data to be able to get data....

I had the basis for the search; those who come after me have the basis for continuation and initiation of future generations of workers in the Work.

No one gave me data; very few had any data at all...I and others similar to myself, because we made the necessity to obtain data, obtained data for the Work. For us, there were no "messengers."

Grace was given from Above. I suppose it is too late now to do anything about it if not, but I *hope* from Above!

In myself understanding did not just happen suddenly. It *grew from a seed.*

For real understanding, it is necessary to have the basis for understanding, which can only be "personal-experience-personally-experienced."

If I had to stand before an artifact to obtain data which was only accessible when I evoked in myself a certain "special state," and moreover, a special state for each type of data, then you can do the same. Having obtained the data, I have become an "organic artifact" from which the data can now be obtained in the same way as I obtained it.

E.J. Gold, *Reimannian Torso*, Bronze,
10-1/4", Edition of 22, 1988.

Chapter Nineteen

THE ULTIMATE ARTIFACT

The ultimate artifact, the organic self, is the exact image of the cosmos within which resides the "I," the exact image of the Absolute but on a smaller scale.

I can foresee but not change my organic destiny; we can make the inner change in our real essential nature, but never the outer; the world remains the same. Some destiny I can force more quickly and some I can avert for some time with the help of the Archangel Gabriel, but only according to the necessity of the Work....

Sit in seance with me for two years until you are able without speech to unlock my personal Soorptkalknian Thought-Tapes. Only this personal experience personally experienced can really prove to anyone the existence of objective work-data. Until you experience this for yourselves, you will never, and should never, believe anything about it.

You should never believe anything I say unless personally experienced—and also personally impartially elucidated—by you. Even then we can expect to be wrong about our objective data now and then.

If you can use my data to get data, then we have accomplished something between us. On the other hand, you may feel uneasy about associating with a man who has spent years which could have been otherwise employed studying with—and listening very hard to—various monuments in one desert or another.

That could be a whole new category of idiot...Monumental Idiot!

If you were struck across the forehead with a big wooden club, you would be more conscious than you are now, but you could not use impressions obtained under these circumstances. Why not use me now? There is no reason to organize expeditions to the farthest reaches of the world in search of the pleasantly exotic....

If you cannot use me as an artifact you will never really understand artifacts. The ultimate artifact is the organic self, the exact image of the cosmos within which resides the "I," the exact image of the Absolute but on a smaller scale.

The organic artifact must someday be opened and its contents understood. This makes all of you, in this respect at least, objectively a virgin.

E.J. Gold, *Bebop Man,* Oil on
Masonite, 60" x 48", 1987.

Chapter Twenty

COATING HIGHER BODIES

Higher bodies are the result of a chemical process which is regulated by breath. Higher bodies give us the opportunity to make our voyage in more than one vehicle.

Just like the ancient alchemist, we must transmute lower metals into gold for the coating of higher bodies.

Higher bodies are the result of a chemical process; we must learn to generate electrical currents much greater than the normal, and change the balance of acidity in the body. Coating of the higher bodies is a process of electrolysis.

The gathering and precipitation of elements for coating, and their transmutation into higher substances, is outlined exactly in some of the more inaccessible alchemical notebooks.

In addition to these substances, the quality of the air must be altered in very specific ways. A book still exists outlining this process; it is called *Hermippus Redivivus,* and was published at about the same time Dr. Johnson made his appearance on this little planet.

Control of it all is a result of activities of the brains, nervous system and glands, all regulated by breath.

We can do nothing to regularize our breath so it can be used for regulation of the chemical factory which produces higher substances from lower raw substances.

We could interrupt the natural tempo of life if we took direct action in the instinctive centrum. But we can regularize breath and put it to work for us by indirect means.

Through moving centrum exercises the breath can be altered naturally to its correct function and then brought into a new way of functioning for the generation and collection of higher transforming substances.

Movements only regularize breath; they do not control or change it in any major way. Very minor adjustments can make breath conform to natural tempos of the organism.

Once breath is regularized according to natural organic rhythms, we can begin to seriously collect substances and transform them for coating our higher bodies.

Of course we do not wish to do so until we have fully crystallized and are satisfied with our "work ego." We would not wish to crystallize our ego formations as they are now; that would be *hasnamos*—a word to describe someone who is irresponsible, unethical and ignorant.

A subjective *hasnamos* is not too bad, but an objective *hasnamos* can cause suffering everywhere.

Work to formulate and formalize the "work ego," in what we can call the essential understanding. You as you are now would not wish for immortality; in one peculiar way you already possess immortality and it has done you no good as yet.

Ordinary immortality is not as we commonly understand it. Life is "one time forever," as if we had only one vehicle.

Higher bodies give us the opportunity to make our voyage in more than one vehicle...We are not trapped in a single cycle of time by having only one form in which to manifest ourselves.

We are not speaking of reincarnation. Reincarnation is not possible without first attaining incarnation. Reincarnation as ordinarily understood does not exist, nor does transmigration of souls.

Frankly, whenever life occurs is the time we have; we always exist during this period of existence from now on, no matter what. But if during this time we have done nothing, then we never do anything. If not *now*, then *never*.

It is not a question of "next time." "Next time" everything will be the same. Nothing different can happen "next time" that did not happen "this time," just as scenes in a film are, considered frame-by-frame, completely static; the actions and outcome will remain constant no matter how many times the viewer may pass through it.

Memories contained in cells give the illusion of having lived before in other lives or other forms....

Imagine life as a tunnel in a spiral form, more or less. From one cosmos higher we are able to see the lifetime connected to itself through another dimension; we do not know nor do we care exactly what dimension it is.

In this higher cosmos everything is frozen; all possible events are connected to each other. We can now see our ordinary men as giant worms frozen in long, spiral twisted forms. Only from outside does it appear to be a worm.

In lower dimensions when we enter and move through—because we can only see one "moment" of its spiral form at a time with ordinary perception— we receive the impression of the passage of time, and seem to be disconnected by time from other sections of space.

We move through this "tunnel of life" frame by frame, like cinema film. There is no movement through time when viewed objectively from a higher cosmos.

Imagine moving through a corridor which has the exact shape of the body at any moment and which spirals, expands and contracts in conformity with the body, and at the same time, the body must move how and where it moves because it is subject to the absolute restraint of its four-dimensional formation.

Nothing you presently know how to do in an ordinary way will free you from this prison. We must learn how to use its own force to overcome it; we can also use the force of consciousness; only by changing being can we grow into another, maybe more conscious, higher cosmic formation.

By expansion we can also change the worm by including other worm-formations, making our four-dimensional body larger and able to hold more data, perhaps even use it wisely for once.

We cannot change anything big. But some things we may be able to change in subtle ways, make some opening.

But one thing at a time. First we must see about the regularization of breath. Imagine the worm as one vehicle, not unlike a motor car. It is your worm and yours alone. It is your "place of arising," and so far, is the only thing you really possess, such as it is.

If, somewhere along the line, we cannot escape from it, how can we hope to escape "next time"? In this sense, there is no reincarnation.

Imagine this vehicle as a motor car from which you cannot get out; it is on a track and always starts and ends at the same place. After a definite number of miles, it stops forever, but still exists as it is.

If we wish to ride this vehicle again, it is possible, but it will always end up the same way. We can select these vehicles from a slightly higher cosmos by viewing impartially the end products.

Subjective experience is unique; time flow is also unique, but it is objectively nonexistent. Time is the impression we have when we move through the giant four-dimensional "slug." If we hope to escape we must have another vehicle; not just another like the first, but an entirely new type of vehicle.

If we are impartial toward the machine, we should be able to easily regularize breath, and in addition do much more to help the chemical factory work as it should, but if we begin to meddle with its natural rhythm, even impartially, we can change it for the worse. More gentle moving centrum work makes indirect changes little by little.

Self-observing always begins with the moving centrum, not mood, thought, cause or effect. We are interested only in pure manifestations, completely impartial, as if observing the activities of a mechanical device. Activities of the machine really have no higher consciousness significance whatever.

Try this: become aware of your breath; in the very first moment you observe without impartiality, the breath has changed. Do not worry about breath now; it is not important because it is not immediate.

Now move your hand and forearm up and down and be aware only of the moving, not of breath. Observe just this one simple "moving centrum phenomenon."

Not complicated. Just the same over and over again. Now notice that the breath has partly regulated itself to accommodate the effort. This is an example in a small way of the effects of moving centrum exercises.

Stare in fascination at this moving centrum manifestation. Put ninety percent of your totality of attention on just this phenomenon; let everything else fall into the dull background.

The machine will remember; trust the machine to continue this movement until you tell it to stop or, if it is very stupid, it will stop eventually all by itself when it becomes bored with repetition.

Now place ten percent of your totality of attention on this movement and ninety percent on how you feel, what you think, your important ideas and most of all on your precious views on everything in general....

Of course let us not forget to fully review all those past actions which put you in a good light, and also those possible future actions which will place you just where you most wish to be...And of course—how could we forget this all-important factor...?

We must also be continually aware of the exact impression we make on others and remedy their ideas of us so that they will not think of us as total nerds.

If we had necessity, we could be continually aware in just the opposite way. Almost all our attention could be on our manifestations in an impartial way. It is just happening all by itself. It is a machine, from which we can expect no more than we expect of any other machine. Just another series of moving-centrum phenomena!

We should be able to impartially observe moving centrum phenomena whenever we wish to; after all, it is just a machine and means nothing in particular; but we cannot observe in the ordinary way, because if we maintain our ordinary view, we are not merely observing a machine, but something which intimately reveals our inmost selves and lowers our carefully constructed artificial self-esteem.

We must be very patient; not be in a big hurry to make organic changes. It took a long time to make this mess; in comparison it will take very little time to repair, but every moment is precious.

If someone tells you to change your breath or even to place attention on your breath for the purpose of some exalted meditation, he is ignorant. Maybe not ignorant about everything, but ignorant about this at least. Even observation is a possible interference in the natural tempo.

The more impartially we observe, the more we are able to observe safely and the more we are able to change later when we take definite action toward the organism.

How can we observe the manifestations of the moving centrum without happening to notice breath as a manifestation of movement? We must remember that breathing is not a manifestation of movement, but of the instinctive functions. The moving centrum is the voluntary part of the motor centrum in general; manifestations of expression of the face, gesture of the extremities and posture are all examples of the moving centrum.

Someday we will take some parts of the involuntary and make them voluntary, but never breath, heartbeat or thoughts, all of which are products of involuntary muscles.

We are not interested in the activities of the instinctive centrum just now; we do not wish accidentally to interfere with the workings of the involuntary part of the organism. Of course, we cannot help occasionally noticing digestion, myo- and cardio-vascular systemic functioning, gastro-intestinal disfunctioning and encephalic mis-functioning.

Certain things are impossible to ignore, but we do not wish to take especial notice of them at this time; we should concentrate our attention in the form of impartial self-observing of moving centrum manifestations.

E.J. Gold, *Le déjeuner,* Acrylic on
Canvas, 32" x 40", 1986.

Chapter Twenty-One

Unlocking artifacts

The Last Supper is an artifact if exactly performed according to its esoteric instruction. The Annunciation, Birth of Jesus, Easter Passion and other Great Voluntary Dramas can also be artifacts and invocations.

Select an object—it does not matter what—and begin to concentrate your attention on it by the technique of "funneling," eliminating more and more inner and outer distractions until you have attained full attention with all three of your ordinary centrums on the object.

I do not include the instinctive or sex centrums in this experiment because they are not used in this way; they are sources of *Force* which can be employed for one aim or another, providing the force behind psychological, emotional and organic activities.

Ordinary organic man seldom if ever is able to use these two sources of *Force*. When accidentally occasionally these centrums release *Force* in the general course of events, we are ordinarily not prepared for what we see and are able suddenly to do, but in a very short time this accidental connection mercifully automatically disconnects itself; and when the connection does not refract, the primate-centered man is generally considered a welcome candidate for special housing at a home for the esoterically bewildered.

For this simple experiment in opening artifacts, the organic form must be very passive in the moving centrum; only those parts of moving-instinctive actually necessary for continuation of life are allowed to continue uninterrupted.

Those parts of the moving centrum needed to concentrate attention on the object continue to be active, *only more so.*

When this has been mastered with very few breaks in attention—that is to say, no inner or outer distractions interfere with the concentrated attention—then we can proceed to the next part of the experiment:

Obtain a photograph of someone you know and concentrate your attention on it in the same way, making full use of thought, emotion, impressions, sensations, memories, associations and imagination; whatever will help you to concentrate your full attention on the person represented in the photograph.

The more centrums you are able to bring into this exercise the more connected they will be; at the same time, concentration on the same aim will give the centrums more balance than they would have in the usual organic way.

It does not matter which emotions exactly happen to be aroused, or what thoughts occur by association. Undoubtedly a parade of subjective emotional and mental associations—and possibly sensing associations also—will automatically arise as we concentrate our attention on the subject, but we should be impartial to details. We are only interested in achieving total concentration of attention.

Whatever thoughts, emotions, emanations, memories, postures, movements, expressions, impressions and subjective ideas the person in the photograph represents, make certain that we make all these "arisings" in ourselves feel-ably tangible....

Then, without looking at the photograph, mentally, emotionally and organically with the moving centrum reconstruct the most vivid possible image of the person in the photograph.

Make it as feel-ably tangible as possible—see, hear, sense and most of all *feel* the presence. This is what is meant by three-centrumed concentration of attention.

Then write the name of that person on a piece of parchment, looking deeply at the letters and sounding the name out mentally syllable by syllable, arousing a three-centrumed visualization of the person in the same way as before, but this time tied to the image and sound of the name.

Then using a name on parchment of someone you have never known, arouse a similar visualization using the sound and sight of the name. This vision should be as clear and exact as if you were in the organic presence of the person, at least in feeling and sensing, if not visually.

Now sit in a chair with another chair before you, facing you.

Looking just in front of the back part of the chair before you, visualize the same person seated in the chair, with his or her eyes closed.

Then slowly have the vision open his or her eyes as if trying to visualize you. In this case, hold the idea that he is present and, as a medium, is trying to visualize you who are not yet present.

At the same time you should be able to sense the emanations of that person, and to sense his presence-of-presence.

Then do this with two chairs before you, side by side; one containing an entity you are attempting to "reconstruct" by visualization, sensing and feeling, and the other containing an entity you definitely know to be benevolent and higher in Reason....

Of course, to determine the Gradation of Reason of another we must either depend on hearsay, or else our Gradation of Reason must be at least the same....

Is this "benevolent entity of a higher Gradation of Reason" something more than human?

Not necessarily; we would invoke a Saint who was once human. But then we must again depend on second-hand data for our information about who is and who is not a Saint.

Unless, of course, we know one or two Saints personally...or know someone who does.

Once we have chosen a higher entity for our "control" who can act for us in a capacity akin to long- distance operator in the *seance,* we can visualize his or her presence in one of the two chairs before us.

Concentrate until, in the dim candlelight, you are able to clearly see both forms, at least in outline. Then have them exchange places several times until they blend into two similar forms containing parts of both more or less evenly distributed between the two.

Once this has been mastered we can proceed to the next part of the experiment:

With a group of four, five, six or seven other serious people—by which I mean serious in their intention, not their manner—be seated at a round wooden table in the same way as you would at an ordinary seance, or around in a circle on a carpet on the floor or seated on cushions....

Write the name of an entity on a piece of parchment and place the parchment in the center of the circle, under the candleholder containing a large candle corresponding in color to the resonating factor of the vibration of the entity in question.

Recite the name aloud, vibrating it in different ways until the sounds make a definite and persisting reverberation in the chamber.

The harmonics and overtones resulting from these vibrating reverberations should continue softly for several hours once the correct resonating factor has been found.

After some practice, the concentrated attention should be perfected to habituality so that just the ordinary recitation of the name and mentally sounding it out will be sufficient.

Exact corresponding atmosphere can be aroused with the use of incense and other smoke; readings can be performed beforehand to suggest the corresponding mood.

It is vital to make the exact corresponding gradation of light and dark.

It does not matter if the participants know anything at all about the experiment as long as they behave themselves, and skepticism—but not cheap cynicism—is healthy in these matters.

Remember that *all* phenomena is illusion. Trance, voice alteration, messages from the Beyond, channeling Cleopatra in modern English—are all hysterical organic reactions to this powerful and uncustomary psychic activity.

Each type will have its own corresponding organic reaction to the *seance.* Some will fall asleep, freeze into stonelike immobility, some will become angry and hostile, some will become sentimental, some afraid, and one or two may even faint or vomit. Hopefully a few will get down to serious business while the others have their little hysterical interludes.

Higher entities do not always answer questions or have conversation. They have their own business here; for them a seance is like an airfield on which they can land temporarily.

Entities of the Work have business of a very special kind all over this little planet.

The Last Supper was just such a seance of a similar kind; it was a late and desperate effort to teach disciples how to invoke and blend themselves into the entity partly represented by the man Jesus, and of which Jesus, Judas and Peter were only parts.

Only joined together with twelve other parts could the entity called "The Christ" manifest corresponding to its higher dimensional morphology. This is why a work group is forced to form itself in the corresponding intimacy and feelings-for-one-another.

The Last Supper requires thirteen organic forms of the human in exact mental, emotional and moving states, although "where two or three are gathered *in my name*," that is, *through the Force of the name itself,* which has healing power, there can be a *partial* manifestation of "The Christ."

The entity called "Jehovah" or "Shem" requires at least ten male humans, called a "minyan," in order to fully manifest. In this case, all participants of the *minyan* must be organic males, just as the manifestation of the entities "Isis" and "Astarte" correspondingly require the presence of female organic formations.

Even in the *hammam*—steam bath—entities sometimes manifest just because all the organic formations are male or all female. Some entities manifest according to the gender of the organic, some do not. Others require exact combinations.

Some entities require added Force and certain substances called "venom" through animal sacrifice. We are not interested in these entities, although we should be aware of their existence *and presence* out-side our sphere of perception.

Some entities are able to partly manifest using smoke supplied by burning certain exact substances over charcoal.

Some entities descend just because some ac-tivity attracts them—certain psychopathic states, for example. Under the right conditions, certain very high entities can be attracted by intentional activities of a very special kind, called "objective magic."

Reconstructions of certain events, whether in-tentionally or not, can also bring down entities and help us to psychometrically penetrate artifacts.

The Last Supper is an artifact if exactly per-formed according to its esoteric instruction. In the same way, the Annunciation, Birth of Jesus, Easter Passion and other Great Voluntary Dramas can be artifacts and invocations.

Some bring a complete manifestation—"miracles or appearances"—while others such as "miracle plays" which were enacted during the Mid-dle Ages bring only partial manifestation—the *emo-tion-of-presence*. Some entities we are able to feel all the time if we become subject to their influence....

A book, if written consciously and with knowledge, is an invocation. When used in an exact setting—such as the *seance* atmosphere—with a candle and no electrical apparatus, it can function as a key to certain artifacts inaccessible in any other way.

A group can sit "in seance" with a book, striving sincerely to understand and bring themselves into the "corresponding-resonating" of the entity connected to this cosmos by the book.

Some books invoke more strongly when read aloud; others invoke nothing. Still others only evoke—bring subjective entities out of one's subconscious—inner entities.

A group reading my writings in an exact setting and in the corresponding mood could evoke the entity who wrote them. Still, my human presence is only one finger of one hand....

To write an effective self-invoking text requires exact knowledge. Ideas are of only minor importance. They serve only to direct the whole attention toward an invoking mood. In this respect, the main impulse should be "the striving to deeply understand" without the belief in ideas-in-themselves.

Our own work has a very small part in the Work as a whole. Perhaps that is all that our necessity has yet produced. In any case it is all we will get in the beginning. Invoking entities for the benefit of the Work does not directly benefit either the entities invoked or those who work to bring them down to our cosmos.

We could call it common-cosmic-order. If we have a machine which needs repair and cannot get inside the machine to repair small parts, then we can—if we know how—occupy or "assume the organic concentration" of one of the inhabitants of the machine, if there are any, and in this case, there definitely are...and they are what we call "organic man."

This is possible only because man is an exact model of the cosmos as a whole....

But for specialized entities which are not like man, it requires several—and sometimes eight or more—men to make a manifestable formation for an entity of higher formation just because these very specialized entities are not exact models of the cosmos as a whole. (In this case "man" refers to a level of creature and not to a species or gender. Questions of sexism and racism are political, and therefore belong wholly to the primate world and have no referent in the Real World.)

In fact, they form cosmoses unique in formation among all possible common-cosmic-concentrations.

Some entities are so specialized in their formation and so different from the Great Cosmos in body and psychological type that they require many thousands of human organic forms for their organic manifestation on planet Earth.

For this purpose they inspire—and then use for their own aims—concerts, religious meetings, political rallies, wars, marches and riots, and so forth.

These entities are very seldom beneficent, but none of the greater entities are neutral in the ordinary sense, although many are impartial.

Think in biological categories: the small entity called *pneumococcus* could represent an entity favorable to the Work. Organically speaking, *pneumococci* does not produce a reaction unless present in a quantity sufficient to upset the ordinary organic balance.

Then what corresponds in nature to man's organic antibodies, those entities malevolent to the Work, insert themselves, so to speak, in the activity. As a result, those entities benevolent to the Work must always be careful not to upset the delicate electrical balance of organic life.

Entities benevolent to the Work are by definition against Nature although only impartially and without malice. They are not, unless provoked, disruptive to Nature.

On the other hand, those entities malevolent to the Work are *for* Nature but not necessarily *with* Nature. They may work against continuation of organic life, but in this they work for Nature in a peculiar and destructive way, as bacteria serve to break down organic matter into nitrogens and other formative materials.

Spiritualist mediums who hold authentic seances call down entities, usually of the animal, vegetable or mineral kingdoms, without knowing exactly what they have done.

This is also true in the practice of Obeah and Voodoo, although the entities in question are in some cases objective animal entities and in other cases—more usually so—inner subjective entities of the deeper, hidden side of the emotional, the "emotional-involuntary," called "Lilith," the first wife of Adam; she is also sometimes called "the dark side of the moon."

A small group will, if operating without real knowledge, only be able to contact more or less harmless entities. Once there is a group of more than eight, there is danger.

In a group of thirteen, very powerful entities can be invoked, and the danger is correspondingly greater.

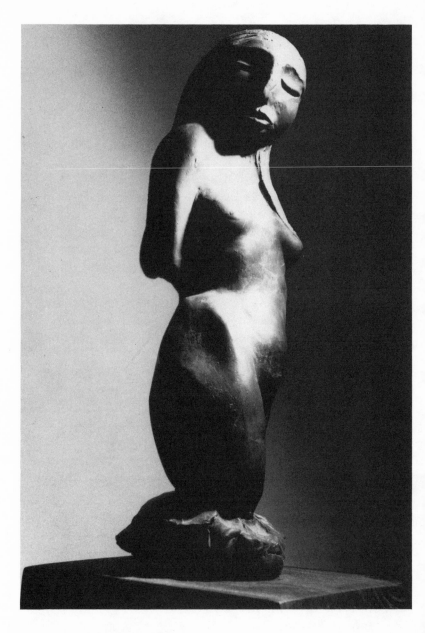

E.J. Gold, *Mayan Lady*, Bronze,
11-3/4", Edition of 22, 1988.

Chapter Twenty-Two

OPEN SESAME

Many artifacts can be found today hidden in ordinary objects: Tarot cards can be psychometrized and one can read everything the images contain. The idea of "Open Sesame" refers to a type of unlocking prayer.

When I first organized expeditions to psychometrically unlock artifacts and monuments I had no idea how to proceed. All I knew was that there was "something" there.

For the first expedition, I made three vows: One vow was to never again earn a living in an ordinary way. The second vow that I made with myself was to do nothing that was natural for me. The third was to never accept the teaching through ordinary means, which made psychometry and invocation a necessity. I knew from prior experience that without the force of necessity there can be no result.

Because of my mission I knew that I could take this vow. The way I constated it to myself was that if Mohammed cannot go to the mountain, because of the force of the mission the mountain must come to Mohammed.

Had I been sent by someone else, I would have been forced to use a different kind of cunning.

I made it harder for myself because I did not have a visible teacher. Not that I had any intention in the beginning not to accept a teacher. I simply did not accept person-to-person data.

Because of the force of my mission, I learned of the existence of higher teachers which we call "entities."

I began as a psychic making "seances" for Theosophists. Those for whom I worked, who were also psychics and mystics, were apparently, as far as I was able to discern, unexplainably disinterested in exploring exactly the meaning of the phenomena with which they were experimenting. They would have some extraordinary result and rather than probe deeper, they became afraid, and backed away from it all.

Picture the situation at that time; having dabbled a little bit in ceremony and ritual, I knew a little something about hypnotism, and thought transference.

I was conducting seances, private readings; I knew a little about the Tarot, how it was constructed, where and when; its original Egyptian form; that is, secret letters an Egyptian priest could write to another by formations of different cards, according to how they were arranged.

And then later, its adaptation by the *Ziganie,* or "gypsies" as a fortunetelling device, and its subsequent spread throughout Europe. It became a craze, and then finally an ordinary card game. Then some of the cards and characters were lost.

In tracing the Tarot back, I came to a dead end. To get through this apparent barrier, I was forced to use "psychometry." By this means I discovered independently the Tarot in the temples and tombs of Egypt, the so-called "posts of initiation."

Then I discovered that each Tarot card, in its true form, could be psychometrized through image, and one could read everything the image contained. So it serves today in its own way as an artifact; even though the card may not be ancient, the image is ancient, connected with the ancient teaching.

At that time I was not interested in verification, only knowledge. I suddenly decided as a result of some of these readings from artifacts on which I intend to elaborate later, to not live the life natural for myself, and to put myself in constant and continual danger, both from physical and also psychical means. This worked very well indeed.

One result of the decision was to travel entirely without a passport for some time. This meant that I had to learn "telepathic hypnosis," to convince officials that I had passport and visas.

Some important artifacts I discovered in private collections. Others are in places that are inaccessible because of beliefs of those guarding the various artifacts. In still other cases, these are inaccessible through stupidity and superstition.

In other cases, they are only accessible through government authorities. I found all this very useful when bringing artifacts into the United States.

I had not yet constated to myself even at this late date exactly what my aim was in the matter of artifacts.

I thought that if knowledge had been placed accidentally in various artifacts—particularly monumental—through terror, death and other forms of negative vibration, that they might perhaps have been placed intentionally somewhere by someone or other, I had no idea just who.

But I knew the idea existed; there were stories which were contemporarily existing versions of ancient myths, such as the story of Ali Baba and the Forty Thieves.

I instantly understood the idea of "open sesame" to mean a type of unlocking prayer and had already seen that certain prayers unlock the healing power of certain shrines...such as the "Jesus Prayer" used at Mount Athos....

Through other types of prayer I thought it might be possible to attract various entities of both Celestial and Diabolical origin, although I had at that time no way of knowing that another important factor was necessary....

Another idea occurred to me that through prayer it must be possible to open—and also to read in an objective way—certain ordinarily inaccessible parts of the psychic self.

I understood that if I could find the keys I would be able to unlock the mysteries of the cosmic and of the psychic at the same time, having already obtained the data from the Emerald Tablet of Hermes: *As Below, So Above.*

As I watched the silent thought-tapes in a Babylonian granite monument, I noticed that, although some recordings had been registered involuntarily through war, famine, plagues and natural disasters, something definitely "otherwise" could be faintly detected behind all this; something which had been almost completely obliterated under the more dominating emotional recordings.

I thought then for the first time that these older thought-tapes might have been placed in the monument by a society very early in contemporary history. I did not know then that very early civilizations had existed long before contemporary man measures the arising of civilization....

In a private collection was a wood carving said to have come from a cathedral in Spain, a carving which was reputed to have great healing powers.

Through examination of this artifact I quickly discovered that many so-called "miracles of healing" take place regularly in the presence of similar artifacts.

Some force is released through emotional prayer along with feelings of hope, faith and love....

Sometimes quite different emotional keys operate healing artifacts and only certain types are able to receive help from them....

This idea, when taken along with the healing ideas of a certain monastery in which I had taken vows when much younger gave me the foundation for a real science of psychic healing.

Later I found that there were two major types of keys corresponding to the voluntary and involuntary types of man, the first corresponding to the 3,6,9 and the second to the musical octave.

There was at that time no categorical data for existing thought-tapes in monuments and other artifacts. Everything about this science was just in its infancy.

My friends and I went everywhere in search of ancient data, and even with a special map of the ancient world we were by no means sure where to search.

In addition, many ancient monuments which had by some miracle survived the ravages of time and man, had been moved from their original locations or buried under tons of sand.

Then we heard that the ancient city Babylon had been uncovered.

The Babylonian ruins divulged for the first time to us that at least one ancient civilization had within its confines one or more esoteric societies in definite possession of the method of implanting Soorptkalknian Thought-Tapes intentionally in artifacts and monuments.

We began the serious study of ancient life and the introduction of man on planet Earth and his subsequent development from a hybrid species into that unique species he has since become.

Soon we were well on our way to every shrine and holy place possible. Travel was limited at this time, but we had no trouble at all gaining access to those places necessary for our aim.

E.J. Gold, *Sisters in the Skin,*
Oil on Canvas, 48" x 60", 1987.

Chapter Twenty-Three

THE INNER CIRCLE
OF HUMANITY

By ourselves we have little force of any real consequence, but as a group, if we are connected, we have more force than any single individual can concentrate.

A group performing similar tasks, movements, and efforts together, and who begin through admiration of each other or of their leader to think alike, take views of the world alike, act alike, dress alike, talk alike and adopt the same postures and gestures begin to sooner or later involuntarily invoke certain entities, particularly entities of the emotional, who are very vampiristic.

It is said that, "By their manifestations, postures and gestures we shall know them"—that is, those who have adopted a group posture and who have become in one way or another addicted to the presence of one or more entities....

We can learn to sort people by manifestations and type. Ordinary man is so subject to entity influences that he cannot voluntarily select his manifestations. Real man is able to not only select his manifestations, but to invent new ones not found among ordinary organic man.

Just for a moment think what it would mean if six human beings could actually be together in a real way, connected in essence by common thought and emotion. This is a big secret of certain esoteric schools which prepare some people for entry into the inner circle of humanity.

By ourselves we have little force of any real consequence, but as a group, if we are connected, we have more force than any one can concentrate.

Picture a glove into which we can fit only one finger, then a glove into which we can fit our whole hand; then view the organic self as a one-finger glove and a functioning and harmoniously blended group as a whole-hand glove. The sum-total of all operating parts of a whole hand is obviously greater than the highest possible gradation of single fingers because it also contains the palm, thumb and wrist. Now imagine a group working in this way.

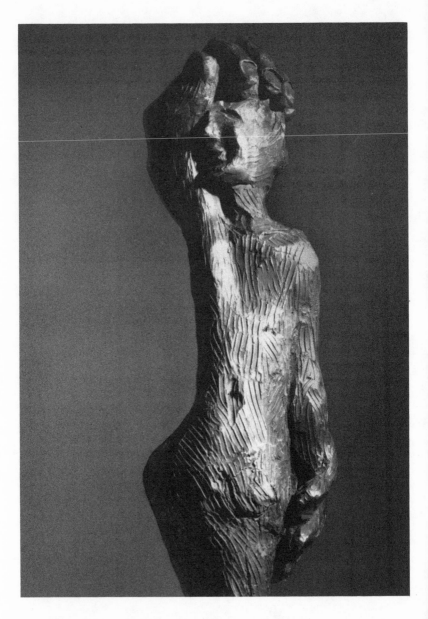

E.J. Gold, *Sculptor Sculpting the Sculptor*,
Bronze, 20", Edition of 22, 1988.

Chapter Twenty-Four

THE DESCENT OF HIGHER ENTITIES

Voluntary group work can make possible not only the descent of a definite entity but also the arising of a new entity in the cosmos.

Any activity which can connect a group of people in the moving, emotional or thinking centrums can at the same time bring down entities, sometimes for the good, and more often for the bad.

In many healing ceremonies where hypnotic repetitions are used, entities claiming to be some benevolent entity or other descend and, while emotional concentrations are aroused and personal discernment is at its lowest, feed on the force resulting from emotional arousal.

Voluntary group work, on the other hand, can make possible not only the descent of a definite entity but also the arising of a new entity in the cosmos, in the same way as the Last Supper produced the Christ.

For the intentional descent of an entity for the Work, we must have a sufficient basis for manifestation so that the entity will be able to temporarily participate in our local planetary business on behalf of the Work.

All temples have as their original basis the same idea: a gathering place for men to connect themselves together temporarily for a common aim—to bring down a benevolent entity.

For this purpose, men have long known even if only intuitively—and schools, some of which have built your cathedrals, have known consciously— various methods of drawing groups of men together through moods induced by light, sound, ritual and architecture.

In the Medieval period in the West, jugglers from Sufi communities in Persia traveled through Europe gathering crowds and, while juggling, would emotionally and mentally align the audience toward a particular state for the descent of an entity.

This important part of the Work is something that "white sheep" definitely do not like.

Those men calling themselves "witches" but who are really pagans in the old sense of the word, gather to form the "organic-receptive" for those entities favorable to organic life on our little planet.

When the various formations of schools and other gatherings are not able, due to superstition or to political pressures, to bring down entities benevolent to organic life, then organic life changes to some degree and war is inevitable.

How can we develop the ability to know how to use these entities for our own work and which ones to help for the Great Work?

Practice, practice, practice. Most of all, experience with impartiality, both personal and impersonal, toward oneself and others.

Do not worry too much when practicing unlocking the ancient thought-tapes from artifacts or calling down entities; good and evil are far beyond your capacity.

Eventually we learn; we can ask a machinist how he does what he does, but he cannot really tell us. On the other hand, he can show us. You practice and after a while—if you survive the inevitable mistakes—you will learn to distinguish one from the other.

Even then, we may never know which, objectively speaking, is which.

E.J. Gold, *Medusa*, Bronze,
4-5/8", Edition of 125, 1988.

Chapter Twenty-Five

IMPRINTING ARTIFACTS

Part of the work is not only to make a "basis" for higher entity manifestation, but to imprint artifacts for future candidates for the Work.

Have you ever walked in the hills and come across rings of stone or old trees and often gone out of your way to visit them without knowing really why?

When we really begin to use a work place it will be a gathering place, a "club of an entirely different kind" and, of course, useless to ordinary man.

It may be useful to locate work centrums in exact locations; lines of Force on the surface of the planet can be connected for work....

Specific entities manifest in definite locations; others are more flexible but only manifest under certain "voluntary conditions."

This is called a "vortex," when a group makes the conditions for voluntary manifestation.

In very ancient civilizations it was called the "Bringing Down", or "Elkdonis." We today would say "helping the Absolute."

We must realize that the ancients knew the future of planet Earth and were able to see what would become of each artifact, although not all societies which made thought-tapes were able to see exactly.

Nostradamus was able to see the whole of the future for man.

In comparison it is easy to see the future for one artifact.

Plain objects and monuments of no great consequence were seen to be more likely to fall into the right hands or to be continually accessible to seekers of truth.

Religious artifacts would become inaccessible due to superstition and power. Most emitting artifacts are not religious articles, although some have become part of religious accumulations through misunderstood formation.

Some are now held within inaccessible monasteries available only to initiates who pass a series of difficult trials. When this is consciously intended and made with future civilizations in mind, then the artifact can remain accessible, but what monastery can survive the ravage of time, which sooner or later grinds every grain?

Part of the work not only forms a "basis" for higher entity manifestation, but imprints artifacts for future candidates for the Work.

It requires a very long time to imprint an artifact, and before anything can be done an artifact must be chosen with knowledge of what may survive.

And then a selection of data must be made. We do not wish to make an artifact with just any old idea in it.

The imprinting of an artifact is a serious matter. The data must be exact. For our own work we cannot be held responsible if we fail or are stupid. But for our data given to future candidates for the Work we are held responsible and accountable.

We must be sure of our data; even if for ourselves it was true, we must be sure it is true in the objective sense.

Figure A

Chapter Twenty-Six

TO DARE

When an artifact is unlocked, a definite cognition occurs which results in the instantaneous transmission of data and sometimes transformation.

Let us start to learn how to psychometrically read an artifact, by assuming the posture in Fig. A. "Settle into" the posture until it feels exact. Only freeze into it for a moment, then release the posture and take a cleansing breath—inhale through the nose, exhale through the mouth. Then again, find the posture. Eventually you will be able to go directly into the exact posture every time.

A real initiated monk can arouse the feeling of humiliation—not humility. Arousing the *emotion of humiliation, freeze into this posture.* The correct emotional key will evoke definite ideas and sensations. The monk's secret for unlocking artifacts is to use various voluntary emotional keys for each artifact, posture or work-effort.

We will use negative emotions at first. Try to feel the emotion of loss. Any emotion can be a key, when used impartially. Activate and hold the emotion impartially. Humiliation, loss, disappointment, anxiety, apprehension, fear; all of these can be used. Sometimes, more than one key is necessary. For example, fear, apprehension and joy are sometimes used all together. Usually one, two or three keys are used.

There are also mental keys. Mentation is the voluntary form of thought. Voluntary emotion is called "mood." There is no word in the English language for voluntary emotion. Ordinary man considers voluntary emotions to be not real emotion. Ordinary man has little love for those who manifest voluntary emotion.

Some artifacts require several moods and mentation to unlock. Sometimes it may be necessary to introduce moods sequentially while holding a posture; at other times it may be necessary to juggle several moods at once. This may be for some a paradox. The key is impartiality. When an artifact is unlocked, a definite cognition occurs which results in instantaneous transmission of data and sometimes transformation.

Try *to pity the awesome while freezing into the posture shown in figure A;* to voluntarily draw down suffering upon oneself *with a mood of disinterest.* This is called "to dare."

There is a certain amount of risk involved in trying to draw down suffering into yourself. Now, get a *feeling of oppressive weight,* then relax and take a cleansing breath.

Figure B

Figure C

Chapter Twenty-Seven

DIE BEFORE YOU DIE

Negative emotions can be burned away by taking on certain postures. If we can change our whole posturing, we will leave ordinary life behind. Transformation and initiation take place by activating artifacts.

Take a cleansing breath. Use sensing to convince yourself that you are looking upward without actually looking upward with your eyes. Voluntarily produce in yourself the sensation of floating on your back, looking upward at the sky. You must be convinced of this, using voluntary sensing, mentation and mood.

Just take the posture shown in Fig. B momentarily. Now, try it again. When we unlock the artifact, it happens instantaneously.

Figure D

Figure E

Eyes open, sense it, do not mentally visualize. Convince the organism that it is upside down, still working with the posture in Fig. B. Now arouse the mood *apprehension* with no visible source of apprehension. The mentation could be intense mental frustration, so packed-with-thought that you are unable to think. Sensing, mood, mentation and posture all together are called a "state."

Experiment with various keys until this postural artifact opens. We may already know the key; sometimes we must discover it. Occasionally verbal commands or sounds are necessary, like "open sesame."

When we activate an artifact we call down the corresponding entity; the entity descends and transformation and initiation can take place. This is real cause and effect when the two are simultaneous and co-creative. In this instance, the invocation of an entity is as unavoidable as rain. Different ideas for keys will occur to you. Become like a lightning rod for knowledge.

Try the posture shown in Fig. C. Without organic reverberation, hold the emotional idea of being hit in the chest. In addition, get the idea of the distance between finger tips being as vast as you are able to imagine. Now arouse the mood resulting from the realization that if you did not exist, events would go on just the same. Be sure you are impartial, but the mood must *not* be impartial.

Mentation for this posture could be, for instance, the *impartiality-of-the-justice-of-it-all*. What justice feels like, tastes and smells like.

Then drop these and arouse the mood *hopelessness* and *despair*. Use this mentation: *the wisdom that you can survive any temporary mood.* The sensation: lifting upwards and slightly back.

Now try the posture shown in Fig. D. Use the mood: *working for another* followed by *watching someone work while you do not.* The sensing: *watching someone work while you do not.* The mentation: *impartial observation of organic sensing and mood.* Do not forget to breathe.

Now freeze into the posture shown in Fig. E for a moment. Have the mood *giddy glee.* Make sure the facial mask is relaxed. The sensing is of *being pulled upward by the wrists.* The mentation: *having just forgotten something that is important, desperate and immediate.*

Now assume a personal posture you often find yourself in, looking at this posture from the views of mood, sensation and mentation. What is the typical primary sensation? Mood? Mentation? Thoughts, ideas, viewpoints, concepts, attitudes are not the self at all.

Like it or not, postures invoke entities with their own memories, views, moods and ideas. Now, take another customary posture. What is the mood, sensing, mentation? Try to identify it. See it as another entity.

Now, another typical posture. Move around in that repertoire of three typical postures. Transitions are important. Entities evoked and invoked through customary involuntary and automatic postures provide man with all his attitudes, knowledge, ideas, viewpoints and moods. See how this has colored your life.

Now take the uncustomary posture in Fig. A. What does this evoke? It is not a customary posture. Let the entity come over you; glimpse it momentarily. This is one purpose of movements, to observe and learn from higher entities. Customary postures evoke only customary—ordinary—knowledge.

Now, another little secret...Working in the garden. Depending on how you work—mood, mentation, sensing—a different entity will descend upon you.

Now, assume the posture in Fig. A again, and arouse a *sullen, nasty, bitchy, mood.* Hold the mentation of *sarcasm, cynicism*...hopeless and despairing. Sense all the organic irritations proceeding. What happened?

Higher entities will not tolerate a negative state. Using these postures along with negative emotions, you can burn them away within yourself permanently.

This is a little secret of life that no one ever can tell ordinary man. If we can change our whole posturing, the old life will die away. This is the real meaning of "die before you die": to choose conscious postures, gestures and expressions, to assume a place in the Work, to leave ordinary life behind, to live a "Work life."

E.J. Gold, *The Dancer*, Bronze,
26-1/2", Edition of 22, 1988.

Chapter Twenty-Eight

CRYPT-O-GRAMS

Each posture is a crypt-o-gram for the manifestations of thousands of entities invoked each day. We wish to know as much about each habitual posture as possible. This is an important technique for self-study.

Code breaking, cyphering. The English love it. We are going to break the *crypt-o-gram* of posture. A crypt means hidden or buried—a crypt-o-gram is an esoteric message, so a posture is a crypt-o-gram. Man is an egotistical swine only because he assumes that all his moods, activities and ideas are his own, that they arise consciously from his own will.

Imagine your lover dead in front of you, then imagine "keening" as Irish and Arab tribespeople do for their dead. With a very slight change in posture you can find the key to the posture of loss and grief.

In primitive societies women are taught formal means to dramatize grief and sorrow, but they must not show concern for themselves; they wish to encourage another husband with their show of loyalty and—in the same spirit as mourners of the ancient world—they add their force to that of the deceased for his voyage in the afterlife. They must attract another husband if they are to survive in their culture.

Now if the husband were to take the posture of *arrogance* and *superiority* it would help the wife to achieve the keening posture and mood. This "objective drama" in which one hand washes the other, is called a tableau. At one time it was considered a high form of drama to create tableaux with emotion.

Keep a catalog of your ordinary postures; draw a simple stick diagram of each, then number or label them something like *the leaner, the slouch, the overseer, the ponderer.*

Accumulate data every day of what you happen to notice about these postures. We wish to know as much about each posture as we can possibly know. This is the real technique for *self-study.*

In dance the whole formation is the invoking force. If there are three on stage, one entity spreads itself through three organic bodies; each person provides one-third of the total morphology of the entity.

In ordinary man, momentary manifestations of many thousands of entities are invoked every day. If we have any power at all, it is the power to voluntarize our postures in order to change what we serve. "Power in the moment" is to change the posture.

Several things work against our aim to escape our slavery. We may enjoy being in familiar postures and emotional states. Additionally, a powerful entity can influence us to continue to assume its corresponding posture and convince us that this serves our purpose either voluntarily or involuntarily.

If we were really serious about work we would assume only those postures which would invoke work entities. Work entities are law-conformable, so we would select fewer and fewer postures. "Will" can be developed so we are able to avoid customary postures and keep ourselves in work postures.

E.J. Gold, *Modi Head,* Bronze,
7-1/2", Edition of 22, 1988.

Chapter Twenty-Nine

BECOMING AN ARTIFACT

An organic artifact is in a very precarious position, because return to the organic is impossible but one is not yet a higher entity, requiring Jacob's Ladder to be able to live and work on a higher scale.

We can become organic artifacts by absorption of "transforming factors," having been exposed to certain artifacts for a sufficient length of time. Sometimes transformation comes first, then data; sometimes a blending of both; sometimes nothing.

In the vicinity of an emitting artifact, it just happens. It is perhaps happening to you, but it is not yet complete; you are not yet fully transformed into an artifact, but it has begun. It is like being poisoned; there is nothing you can do to get rid of it. I have poisoned tens of thousands just by sitting in cafés.

Change takes many years of contact. The data alone is not important. *It is the accumulation of emissions from the artifact which causes transformation.*

To become an involuntary artifact is to sit between two stools. One is no longer of the organic, nor is one a higher entity. It is a painful position. One is forced to create other artifacts to replace oneself in order to free oneself. After we have successfully replaced ourselves, we know how to escape organic life and can begin to do so by voluntarily creating organic artifacts such as we have become.

It is in this way to my benefit to help you complete your transformation into an artifact.

It is a slow process. Each transformation produces a greater need for the "next dose," as with a drug addict. The hope is always that the next "fix" will be permanent.

An organic artifact is in a very precarious position because he cannot return to the organic, but he is not yet a higher entity. He must learn to use Jacob's Ladder and go higher.

Also the longer we work together the more dangerous it is for me. If Mother Nature ever catches up with me....

Mother Nature produces thousands of seeds in the organic, but "Father Nature" also produces thousands of seeds of his own kind. It is in Father Nature's best interests for us to build the higher. Father Nature is governed by the Law of Three, while Mother Nature is governed by the Law of Seven. No one including Father Nature can take you out of the lower; self-initiation, your own attention and will producing something real from within yourself, is the only real means of escape from the psychological and emotional dependence we involuntarily develop through our exposure to the inexorable will-and-attention eroding force of primate life.

Once we have self-initiated to a certain point, only then does assistance from Father Nature become possible. The arising of an entity with even the *possibility* to escape Mother Nature is purely accidental.

Organic man dies in organic life, but an *artifact* cannot die in organic life. He can only evolve beyond organic life, die before he dies...For organic man this idea has no meaning.

Once we have become an artifact there is no other choice for us.

An artifact is eternal within the limits of the solar system. Without a completed higher body and direct help from above, we are stuck in the eternal, and have no guarantee that we will be able to work toward anything higher.

We may find ourselves in a position where we really need help, and cannot ask for it.

The excruciating pain of being suspended between two stools forces us to involuntarily create artifacts until we succeed in replacing ourselves. This process will give the data for escape from organic life.

Small objects make better artifacts, objects that will be cherished from generation to generation.

In this sense it may be more useful to make an artifact out of a "Teddy Bear." We can make an artifact of anything, it does not matter what. It can even be objects such as clothing...a shoe, book, music, pen, anything at all....

There are two very important laws for this idea: Law of Conservation and Law of Economy.

When we first become an artifact and accept the situation, we begin work by introducing others to artifacts so that through exposure, they may be influenced and eventually become artifacts.

At this point work is difficult because we are not yet fully developed and cannot satisfy the needs of a real addict. But by working in this way, our emissions become stronger and eventually we develop a working magnetic centrum; then whoever has this special need will be drawn like bees to nectar.

E.J. Gold, *The Hermit*, Pastel,
9-1/2" x 12-1/2", Sennelier, 1972.

Chapter Thirty

CELLULAR DATA

Knowledge is a definite cellular substance, sometimes intentionally formed by resonance. Cells are erased and data transferred, then introduced through food, drink or air.

It is possible through accumulation of cells which are "data-corresponding" to psychometrically have a great body of data available on many different subjects. In this manner we can piece together much organically stored information which otherwise would be unavailable directly.

We can form a "cellular community" of data-corresponding cells. Cells come to us almost completely at random. The chance of accumulation of these cells is both enhanced and limited by geographic location. We can increase our odds of obtaining particular data cells by drinking, for example, Japanese beer.

With this, the chances of accumulating "Zen cells" of ancient sages increases somewhat.

Those cells produced or altered from ordinary food and air are made of organic cells which either were or were not associated with cells in which we might be interested.

This is why in ancient times it was customary to cook and eat the body of one's teacher, and why certain so-called "primitive" tribes hold it to be a great prize to be allowed to eat the heart of one's enemy, although this idea is degenerated from a real idea from a very high civilization of the Golden Age. Even so, it is more correct than the ideas of contemporary science in the domain of literary and electronic media accumulation of data-and-knowledge.

Knowledge is a definite cellular substance, sometimes intentionally formed by resonance. Cells are erased and data transferred, then introduced through food, drink or air. One must, of course, be able to have access to data contained in cells for this transference or "baraka" to be of any real use.

If you cannot read the data of cells, to eat at my table is useless. We serve *prospero*—whole bread as made and used by very high ancient civilizations— and *schnapps* only to those who have become in themselves "organic cellular mediums."

Once you know it can be done, you can find a way to do it. A lot of unaccounted-for memories of the past we can only attribute properly to cellular data. We can get a taste of cellular data and begin to use it the more we recognize it.

I have a hobby—I collect a certain domain of work-data, like a butterfly collector. Some of my butterflies provide work data.

INDEX

182

Tibetan, 51
Time, definition of, 117
Trance, 128
Transformation, 102, 156, 161, 169 ff.
Transmission, 85, 98
Type, 144

Venom, 129
Vesalius, 100
Vibration(s), 91, 127
    negative, 138
Visualization, 125
Vodka, 77
Voodoo, 133
Vortex, 152

Wadi Ghesub, 26
Will, 167
    definition of, 93
    for self-initiation, 170-171
Work, the, 85, 99 ff., 106, 109, 128 ff., 148, 152
Work
    data, 177
    ego, 114
    Great, 149
    group, 147
    life, 163
    on self, 101

Yezidi
    District, 69 ff.
    shrines, 70

ABOUT THE AUTHOR, E.J. GOLD

E.J. Gold is a true voyager in the heroic tradition, always keeping the highest aims and the purest ethics close to his heart throughout his explorations. His life story is a veritable odyssey through contemporary society, an adventurous journey to unlock inner secrets which he learned to skillfully communicate to others.

Mr. Gold had what could only be called a "culturally privileged" childhood in the sense that his parents' New York apartment was a meeting place of the New York intelligentsia of the time who gathered with his father Horace L. Gold, founding editor of *Galaxy* (science fiction) magazine. As a young child he met visionary writers, artists and scientists. With an early penchant for writing and all the arts, he began—as a teenager—to publish science fiction stories, to write film scripts and to work with his father on *Galaxy* magazine.

A gifted painter and sculptor, Gold moved to Los Angeles in the late 50's, studied art and cinema there, and emerged in the '60's as a respected sculptor in the California Nine group. In Hollywood, he wrote scripts for movies and television shows and performed in his own right as a comedian and a dramatic actor. With a lively interest in classical and jazz music, he professionally produced and engineered records for several major artists during the lively '60's, and he sat in with many bands in New York and Los Angeles jazz clubs.

Versatile and talented as he was, E.J. Gold was not satisfied to settle into a safe niche as a successful artist. He worked to master every art and communication field he could get his hands on, always using one form to complement his knowledge in another form—culminating in his impressive success in penetration of the subject of personal transformation. Beginning in the late '50's, he worked with people in group situations to research and test the entire range of approaches to transformation.

Having begun before spiritual life was big business, E.J. Gold is still, twenty-five years later, working actively in this field. He is now internationally known as an originator of contemporary processes of transformational psychology—a teacher's teacher—and as a masterful proponent of proven ancient methods of "labyrinth voyaging" and voluntary evolution. A writer's writer as well, he's a longtime member of SFWA (Science Fiction Writers of America), a master of satire and author of more than twenty books on subjects ranging from natural childbirth and conscious dying to shamanism and techniques of mystical vision.

According to colleagues, fans and reviewers of Mr. Gold's books, his latest series, beginning with *The Human Biological Machine as a Transformational Apparatus*, is his most significant contribution to date to the literature of mysticism, consciousness and meditation. His literary specialty is the practical use of long-atrophied classics, masterpieces of ideas presented with the utmost force and clarity, ideas not spun from intellectual abstraction but tested, lived and communicated from the heart.

With *Practical Work on Self* and *Visions in the Stone*, he is taking a step causing many of his students to gasp by releasing in public format—no longer as privately-issued small-group study materials—the most sensational and profound of his discoveries over twenty-five years of research on inner awakening and transformation. Closer than ever before to the pearl-beyond-price, the heart's understanding of the never-truly-lost knowledge of life's purpose, E.J. Gold invites discerning readers everywhere to sample the banquet of his new books and take whatever they can use for their own nourishment.

FOR FURTHER STUDY . . .

Books by E.J. Gold

Practical Work on Self
Visions in the Stone: Journey to the Source of Hidden Knowledge
American Book of the Dead
The Human Biological Machine as a Transformational Apparatus
Life in the Labyrinth
Creation Story Verbatim
The Lazy Man's Guide to Death & Dying
The Invocation of Presence
Secret Talks on Voluntary Evolution
The Joy of Sacrifice

Books by Other Authors

Self-Completion: Keys to the Meaningful Life by Robert S. de Ropp
The Dream Assembly by Zalman Schachter-Shalomi
Living God Blues by Lee Lozowick
*The Golden Buddha Changing Masks: Essays on
    the Spiritual Dimension of Acting by Mark Olsen*

Talk of the Month

*A journal of work ideas featuring transcriptions of lectures by
E.J. Gold. For subscription and back issue information write to
Gateways.*

Spoken Word Audio

Inner Awakening and Transformation
The Rembrandt Tape
The Cogitate Tape by John Lilly, M.D., and E.J. Gold

Music from E.J. Gold, the Hi-Tech Shaman

Shaman Ritual I: 'Way Beyond the Veil
Shaman Ritual II: Golden Age
Mystical Journey of the Hi-Tech Shaman
Live at the Philharmonic I
Live at the Philharmonic II
The Cogitate Tape
Adventures of the Hi-Tech Shaman
How I Raised Myself from the Dead
Journey Through the Great Mother
Dance of the Hi-Tech Shaman
Bardo Dreams
Venus Rising

Music by Other Gateways Recording Artists

Life in the Labyrinth by Jimmi Accardi
The Wheel by Martin Silverwolf
Where You Are by Drew Kristel and the Not Always
    North American Drum Core

Video

The Movements Series
G. en Amerique
Hooray for Hollywood
Revenge of the Fly
Godfan
An Evening Shot to Hell with Parker Dixon

188

Dear Reader of *Visions in the Stone:*

This book is the map of a territory, or domain, for your use—don't mistake it for the territory itself.

Since it includes instructions for a few simple preparatory tests and experiments, it can point you toward a usually-invisible gateway to a great inner adventure. If you are one of those intrepid readers with a taste not only for the travelogue, but also for the journey itself—you may be ready for further explorations into the use of emitting artifacts.

Apart from the study materials listed, there is an extensive series of private publications that provide further background and an advanced course of preparation for the Work. There is also information available on the art of psychometry and the psychometrizing of art objects, both ancient and contemporary.

For a current listing of resource materials, a catalog of art works by E.J. Gold available for you to purchase, or information on setting up a program of preparatory work along the lines mapped out in *Visions in the Stone,* contact Gateways at this address/phone:

GATEWAYS
BOOKS & TAPES
PO Box 370 Nevada City, CA 95959
Tel: (916) 272 - 0180
Fax: (916) 272 - 0184
Orders: (800) 869 - 0658